Praise for *The Lighthouse*

Glenn Daman brings a pastor's heart to the task of responding to God's immeasurable character and relating to Him in His majestic compassionate grace. Spending twenty weeks pondering the beauty of God will result in a deepened experience of His present reality. Take and read and grow deep in the wonder of our loving Lord.

Gerry Breshears, PhD
Professor of Theology
Western Seminary, Portland

Glenn Daman's twenty-week devotional focuses on God's character. Each day builds upon this theme, providing a tightly woven tapestry that helps readers see God more clearly.

Personally, I plan to re-read this multi-layered devotional again and again, gleaning from Glenn's excellent work. This devotional has already become a foundational part of my daily quiet time!

I recommend this devotional to anyone wanting to know more about the nature and the characteristics of God. It is an excellent tool for those wanting to grow deeper in their relationship with God. The more we learn of God's radiance, the more we are changed into His glorious likeness!

Dr. Jeffrey Clark
Global Rural Researcher
International Missions Board & Wheaton College

Glenn Daman has written a wonderful twenty-week devotional guide focusing readers on the character of God. It reminds me of A.W. Tozer's Knowledge of the Holy in scope, but it reflects twenty-first century Christianity rather than the 1950s. It is balanced theologically, and it is written for the believer who wants and needs a practical dose of God's Word! I appreciated Glenn's linkage of a teaching introduction for each weekly concept along with bite-sized daily readings to help us think more completely about the character concept. Pastor Glenn reminds us: "God's purpose is not just to save us from sin but also to an eternal relationship with Him. Eternal life is not just living forever in heaven; it is to enter into a lasting relationship with God that begins now and is culminated in heaven. God desires to be a part of our life. He redeems us to be transformed into the image of His Son. He wants to change us." This would be a great book for a congregation to read and reflect upon God's character together. I recommend it.

Rev. Patrick A. Blewett, D.Min., Ph.D.
Dean at A.W. Tozer Seminary and Special Projects at
Simpson University
Author of *Discovering Our Roots, Establishing Our Legacy*

Glenn Daman writes as a pastor, equally familiar with the text of the Bible and the struggles of people. These reflections were born out of his love for his church as they lived through a pandemic. It was a gift to them and will be a gift to any sincere reader. This twenty-week meditation on the attributes of God will do just what the title suggests -- it will provide a guiding light through dark times.

Scott Reavely, DMin
Lead Pastor, New Life Church
Board of Trustees, Western Seminary

Glenn takes us deeper into the revelations of knowing who our God is. You will delight in the many gems of truth that will stir your heart to love and trust your Heavenly Father more and more each day.

This devotional book will be the spark that lights a fire of greater passion to know, love and talk with your Heavenly Father.

This book shouts the radiance of God's character. Each day's devotional will shine God's love, care, holiness, protection and blessing on you. God is true to what He says about Himself and Glenn beautifully reveals deep hidden secrets into the majesty of His most Holy name.

Each devotional will bring encouragement to your heart and build you up in your faith. Truth will resonate in your heart, soul, mind and Spirit. It will be life changing. You will not want to miss a day. This is a book of HOPE!

Everyday Glenn will take you deeper into the depths of the riches of the wisdom and knowledge of God. Each day you will be drawn closer to God as you learn something new of His nature. You will sense Him speaking to your heart that He is true to His nature, no matter what the circumstance. Your fears will turn to faith as you trust in His Holy Name.

Fern Nichols
Founder Moms In Prayer International
Author of *Mom's Little Book of Powerful Prayers, Every Child Needs a Praying Mom, Moms in Prayer: Standing in the Gap for Your Children, Prayer from a Mom's Heart, and When Moms Pray Together: True Stories of God's Power to Transform Your Child*

The deeper you traverse into a person's character the more you will come to know the qualities that draw you to that person or that make you struggle with that person. When it comes to the person of God, the more you know Him the more you will be drawn to the beauty and majesty of His character. Glenn Daman has written an incredible resource in The Lighthouse, to help you know the character of God more deeply. My prayer as you use this resource is that you would be continually transformed by the beauty and glory of God.

Josh Laxton, PhD.
Co-Director of the Wheaton College Billy Graham Center
Co-Regional Director of Lausanne Movement North America
Wheaton College Billy Graham Center
Author of The Bible in 52 Weeks for Men: A Yearlong Bible Study, and
Crisis Leadership From a Christian Perspective (with Ed Stetzer).

"I am excited about recommending Glenn's devotional, "The Lighthouse" to all my fellow residents of rural America. Glenn has a heart for rural America and is concerned about ministering to the people who live there. This 20 week devotional is first of all God centered. As one goes through this study, one should have a clearer view of who God is. This study is not just a another study of the attributes of God but is practical in that it draws the reader into an awareness of the stability that the personhood of God gives us who depend on Him during our hard times. This is so relevant to the rural American who is facing a sense of marginalization because of the current pandemic and for that matter future trials as well. This study will give hope to a section of society that is often overlooked. If you think that you are in an area of the world that is forgotten during this challenging time, I encourage you to go through this this study and be encouraged that God almighty has not forgotten you and is shining His light in your area as well. Remember " In all your ways acknowledge Him, and He shall direct your paths" ~ Proverbs 3:5-6. As you go through this study, let the light of God's word be the light that directs you through whatever situation you find your self in. Thanks Glenn for shining the light of God's word on our situation and giving us the Hope that only comes from a personal relationship with God through Christ."

Jon Hansen
Assistant Director
Village Missions

The Lighthouse

FINDING SECURITY IN THE RADIANCE OF
GOD'S CHARACTER

Glenn C. Daman

CrossLink Publishing
RAPID CITY, SD

Daman/CrossLink Publishing
1601 Mt Rushmore Rd. Ste 3288
Rapid City, SD 57701
www.CrossLinkPublishing.com

Ordering Information:
Quantity sales. Special discounts are available on quantity purchases by corporations, associations, and others. For details, contact the "Special Sales Department" at the address above.

The Lighthouse/Glenn C. Daman. —1st ed.
ISBN 978-1-63357-413-7
Library of Congress Control Number: 2021948363

To the Church Family of River Christian Church
for their acceptance of my faults,
for their forgiveness of my failures,
for their encouragement in my service,
and their faithfulness in the ministry of Christ.

Contents

Acknowledgments

These devotionals were written to encourage people during the COVID-19 pandemic. COVID-19 was a defining moment for the nation and for the people as the events unfolded. Thus, the focus of the devotionals was to provide perspective and encouragement for people as they felt the weight of the pandemic and the upheaval it brought.

I would like to especially thank the congregation of River Christian Church, who remained faithful to the church and committed to the ministry during this challenging season.

I would like to thank my wife, Becky, for her continued support and partnership in ministry. For the past thirty-five years she has been a faithful servant of Christ and has been my most important asset in ministry.

I would also like to thank John Reaney and Debbie Robison for their willingness to read the manuscript and provide invaluable input in the writing of this book.

Last, I would like to thank Rick Bates and Crosslink Publishing for their willingness to publish this material. I would also like to thank Matthew Doan for his superb editorial skills.

It is my prayer and hope that this book will be an encouragement to those who are facing struggles in their life by providing them a greater understanding of the nature of God, who brings security and hope in a troubled world. Ultimately my prayer is to glorify God and honor Him in all that is written, for there is no greater value than knowing Christ and being found in Him (Philippians 2:8–11).

The Hope of the Lighthouse

Finding A Safe Haven in God

T he morning started as a perfect day for sailing. The seas were calm, and the sky was clear, and the sailors anticipated crossing one of the most dangerous waters in the ocean. To reach the port's safety, they would have to cross the treacherous bar known for destroying ships and drowning men. Throughout their voyage, they had faced death in the storms. However, the weather was in their favor today, and safety seemed reachable. Then, just when security was within reach, the weather suddenly and drastically changed. The clouds turned dark, and the winds began to blow. The sailors' nightmare descended upon them; the unexpected, violent tempest suddenly turned the calm waves into deadly breakers. The sailors soon found themselves thrown about by the violent waves as the ship began to founder. The sky turned dark, and the night encompassed them. Even the most seasoned and salty sailor among them began to quake as the terror of the violent gale swept them up in a cauldron of crashing waves. As night enveloped them, despair overwhelmed them. Unable to see where they were and where they were going, they lost hope of navigating past the rocky shore to the safety of the harbor. Unable to chart a course, they were driven blindly about by the waves. All they could hear was the crashing cacophony of waves upon the rocky outlets, which belligerently beckoned them to their doom.

Suddenly, just when they lost hope, a guiding light penetrated the dark: a lighthouse. A place of security and safety which gave them perspective and clarity in their course. Unable to see the harbor, the lighthouse provided them direction to lead them safely home. For the sailors, the lighthouse was more than just a light upon the shores: it was the beacon of hope, the place of security, and the pilot to lead them when the storms assaulted their ship. The lighthouse was the promise of safety, the hope for the sailor otherwise lost in the darkness.

Life turns at a moment's notice. When trials and adversity strike, they burst in unexpectedly and unanticipated. Suddenly, life changes from carefree and confident to uncertain and insecure. Like a sudden storm upon the ocean, the waves turn ominous and the clouds foreboding. While we know that life will bring sorrow, we are never fully prepared for it when it breaks swiftly upon us. We do our best to avoid the unavoidable. But we still face the reality of suffering. In those times, like a ship cast upon turbulent waters, we need a lighthouse to give forth its light and bring hope, guidance, and perspective.

We find meaning and purpose in life when God becomes the focus of our attention and desire. In Philippians 3:7–11, Paul expresses what we need to remember—namely, that what we value is revealed by what we are willing to sacrifice to attain it. How we spend our money, our time, and our energies all reveal our value system. For Paul, that which had the most outstanding value was the knowledge of Christ. In comparison to knowing Christ, everything else becomes secondary and insignificant. Charles Spurgeon, the renowned preacher of the 1800s, wrote, "The highest science, the loftiest speculation, the mightiest philosophy, which can ever engage the attention of a child of God, is the name, the nature, the person, the work, the doings, and the existence of the great God whom he calls his Father."[1] This is especially true during times of sorrow.

Adversity reveals what is important to us and what we value. It also demonstrates our view of God. When our God is small, problems become overwhelming; when our God is big, our problems become insignificant. The issue is not the size of the struggles we face; rather, the real issue is the size of the God in whom we trust. In times of struggle and pain, we quickly focus upon the problems that overwhelm our thoughts and emotions. We discover the answer to dealing with the complexities of life by renewing our perspective of God and keeping Him the focus of our attention. God does not promise us freedom from the effects of a fallen world where death and decay become part of life. Instead, He promises us to use the circumstances of life to reveal Himself to us in ways that make those circumstances fade. God uses every struggle in life to display Himself in new ways so that we might be conformed to His image.

A vital part of growing in the knowledge of Christ comes through our suffering. To participate in the life of Christ involves participating in His suffering and death. If, suffering is God's tool to instill the character of Christ within us, then our pain brings a new understanding of Christ and what it means to live for Him. To live with the paradox of suffering in the Christian life, we must live with a renewed vision of God. This is why it is critical that when we go through seasons of pain, we focus on the character and being of God, for we discover our life in Him. As you go through this journey, find a new understanding of who God is and allow the knowledge of God's character to transform your perspective of the circumstances you face.

While the sailor had the lighthouse, what do we look to to guide us when our lives are assailed by a storm that threatens our well-being? Where do we turn to find hope and direction when

1. Charles Spurgeon, quoted in J.I. Packer, *Knowing God* (Maddison: Intervarsity Press, 1973), 13.

life becomes an uncontrollable storm? The lighthouse that serves to guide us and protect us, giving guidance and perspective in confusing times, is the character and being of God. Christ states in John 8:12, "I am the Light of the world; he who follows Me will not walk in the darkness but will have the light of life." When we can no longer see clearly what is before us, we must look to the person of God. In our understanding of God, we find the anchor for our souls.

Finding Our Security in God

The Lord is my rock and my fortress and my deliverer, my God, my rock, in whom I take refuge. My shield and the horn of my salvation, my stronghold.
Psalm 18:2

Understanding and meditating upon the attributes of God is more than just theological jargon. God invites us to know Him and to delve deep into the exploration of His character and being. God desires to be known; He desires that we search for an understanding of Him. The Infinite invites the finite to explore the wonders of His being. Scripture reminds us continually that we can never fully comprehend God. As the psalmist says, "Great is the LORD and greatly to be praised, and His greatness is unsearchable" (Psalm 145:3). This leads us into the greatest paradox of Scripture, the God who cannot be known completely invites us to search and discover who He is. The ultimate purpose of our salvation is not merely the deliverance from the ravenous effects of sin and the eternal judgment it brings; the purpose of our salvation is to enter into a never-ending relationship with the God of the universe so that we might be "increasing in the knowledge of God" (Colossians 1:10). God does not hide behind the shroud of His holiness but instead reveals Himself in all that He does.

First, He has revealed Himself in His creative works. He has placed the stamp of His character in all that He does. "For since the creation of the world His invisible attributes, His eternal power, and divine nature, has been clearly seen" (Romans 1:20). The masterpiece reveals the artist. With each stroke of the brush, the artist gives expression on the canvas of the depth of His character. So, throughout all creation, with each stroke of His creative brush, we see the self-revelation of God. We see His majesty in the beauty and brilliance of a sunset. We see His power in the shaking sound of thunder. We see His infinite being in the expanse of space. The language of creation is universal and constant: "The heavens are telling of the glory of God, and their expanse is declaring the work of His hands. Day to day pours forth speech, and night to night reveals knowledge. There is no speech, nor are there words; their voice is not heard" (Psalm 19:1–3). Just as we see God's character throughout the pages of Scripture, we also need to see God in all aspects of creation.

Second, He has revealed Himself in His Word. The Bible is more than a compilation of religious writings; it is the autobiography of the living God, penned by Him to reveal to us who He is. While creation brings to light God's creative power, in His Word we find that He is a relational God who desires to be involved in His creation. His Word gives us insight into His moral being to understand what He values and who He is. Thus, His words "are more desirable than gold, yea, than much fine gold; sweeter also than honey and the drippings of the honeycomb" (Psalm 19:10).

Third, and greatest of all, He has revealed Himself by coming in the flesh to walk among us. Christ's incarnation is the ultimate expression of God's desire to be known by us. "And the Word became flesh, and dwelt among us, and we saw His glory, glory as of the only begotten from the Father full of grace and truth" (John 1:14). To see Christ is to see the Father. This is the divine invitation of the gospel. It is not just about freedom from the guilt of sin. It is about entering into an eternal relationship in which God invites us to know Him and explore the depths of His being.

It is this knowledge that gives us confidence and comfort in life's struggles. God is the one constant, the one eternal thing, the one being that is certain in a world that is uncertain and transitory. When confronted with tragedy, adversity, and struggles, we strive to find security. We want something to grip that remains unshakeable. However, that which is certain is not found in our circumstances or even our possessions, but the living God.

Day 1
Finding Security in an Insecure World

Read Isaiah 40:1–8

The grass withers, the flower fades, but the word of God stands forever. Isaiah 40:8

Daily we are reminded of the uncertainty of life and the frailty of man. We are continually being reminded that there is nothing secure in this world. For all our scientific knowledge, technological advancements, and economic prosperity, a microscopic virus can bring us a sense of complete helplessness. When a crisis strikes, especially on a national scale, we become obsessed with reading the news and following the latest reports. However, the more we know, the more apprehensive we become. We are reminded of how transitory life is. As Isaiah points out, our life is frail from the very beginning, and our vibrancy soon fades. We think of the frailty of a baby and the feebleness of the elderly, but the time between the two is brief. In our youth, we believe that time is endless, that we have an eternity to accomplish our goals and dreams. Yet, time quickly passes, and the vibrancy of youth is soon lost to the onslaught of age. The strong young man soon becomes the broken and hunched over elderly. And the dreams that guided us when we were young become lost in the fog of forgetfulness.

In comparison to eternity, our lives are nothing more than a speck. Consequently, the sage in Ecclesiastes reminds us of the urgency of maintaining our focus upon God. "Remember also your Creator in the days of your youth, before the evil days come and the years draw near when you say, I have no delight in them" (Ecclesiastes 12:1). The wise is not the one who makes great plans and dreams abundant dreams. Instead, the wise is the one who recognizes how quickly the evil days come because the vibrancy of youth soon fades as the body slowly dies. The brevity of life is not to lead us to despair but to the importance of seeking the basis for hope and security that moves us from the realm of insecurity and brevity to the realm of security and eternity.

Nevertheless, even amidst all the uncertainty, there is a place and source of security: the Scriptures. The Word of God remains unchanged and relevant forever. Furthermore, the message of the Bible not only stays true and unchanging; it is the source of discovering the hope of eternity. It not only remains forever but through its message, it imparts eternal life to us. This becomes our comfort. The psalmist writes in Psalm 119:76, "O may Your loving-kindness comfort me, according to Your word to Your servant." While it is essential to remain informed, we should not become fixated and preoccupied with the latest news. Instead, we need to become focused upon the study of God's Word. His word is steadfast and eternal, and the promises of God remain valid for all time. It will bring us comfort, peace, and encouragement. To live without apprehension, limit the amount you read the news and spend more time reading the Bible.

Day 2
Finding Security in God's Control

Read Isaiah 46:8–11

Declaring the end from the beginning, and from ancient times things which have not been done, saying, 'My purpose will be established, and I will accomplish all My good pleasure.' Isaiah 46:10

One of the greatest fears that grips us is the fear of the unknown. We want to be in control of our lives and the events that affect us. To live in the realm of the unfamiliar is to live in the arena of ambiguity and confusion. As a result, we are always seeking to gain some sense of order and meaning in life. The most troubling thing about adversity is that it confronts us with our powerlessness to control the events of our life. We make plans for the future, only to have those plans interrupted by circumstances that we did not anticipate and cannot control.

In the realm mysterious our imaginations run amok. In our minds, we can dream great dreams, but we also can imagine great evils. As a child, we do not fear the darkness; we fear the things we imagine are shrouded by the night. As we become adults, we may no longer fear the dark, but we still fear the unknown. Our minds play tricks on us via the "what if . . .?" game. Our most significant worries, the thoughts that keep us awake at night, are fears of the unknown lying ahead, for we cannot control what we do not know.

In these days, when the circumstances surrounding us seem out of control, we can have absolute confidence that God is still orchestrating the events according to His eternal purpose. There is nothing that happens within the universe, including our lives, that escapes His notice. No event is arbitrary or haphazard in His sovereign plan, as He moves all things according to His purpose and end. This is true for all of history, from the movements of nations to our own individual lives. This is why Paul could state, "God causes all things to work together for good to those who love God" (Romans 8:28). Not that all things are good (pandemics and sickness are not good), but this means that God is orchestrating everything within our lives to accomplish His purpose, which is to "conform us to the image of His Son" (Romans 8:29).

Furthermore, God has not hidden His plan from us. In His Word, He not only tells us what He does, but He also assures us that He will do it. In His Word, we find the shroud of darkness removed and the clarity of day bringing to light what God is doing in our lives. We discover God's plan for us. Therefore, when you go through adversity and the trials of life, trust in God's sovereign control, knowing that He is indeed at work in your life and will use these events to transform you into His image—which is the greatest good of all.

Day 3
Finding Security in the Hope of God

Read Psalm 42

As a deer pants for the water brooks, so my soul pants for you, O God. . . . Why are you in despair, O my soul? And why have you become disturbed within me? Hope in God, for I shall again praise Him, for the help of His presence. Psalm 42:1

David knew the pain of trouble. Not only did his enemies seek his life, but he also had to flee Jerusalem when his own son sought to usurp the throne. Psalm 42 is a psalm written in troubled times. Throughout the psalm, David speaks of deep troubles and anguish. We find the writer in the throes of not only emotional depression, but spiritual depression as well. He reflects on the joyous occasions when he sang the praises of God . . . but these songs no longer bring comfort, but despair. In verse 7, he compares his circumstances to breakers and waves crashing over him, threatening to drown him in the waters of the deep. But these waves of trials are not coming from others, but God! Now, instead of his life being filled with praise, it becomes filled with tears (v. 3). The taunt of his adversaries, "Where is your God," becomes his cry of despair. In his hour of great need, he wonders, "Has God forgotten me?!" (v. 9). When we face the struggles of life, this becomes our anthem as well. We not only question God's protection, but we even begin to question His presence and goodness. Like the psalmist, we lose hope as the trials mount.

Yet, we see woven throughout the psalm not only David's deep desire to fellowship with God, but also his rock-solid confidence that God would be with him during his time of trouble. Rather than his depression leading him to deny God, it causes him to reaffirm his trust in God and his confidence that God is still faithful. He expresses his deep thirst to know God, for God is his hope, God is present with him, and God commands his loving-kindness to be with him and be his help. Consequently, even as David is going through his despair, he finds God to be his comfort and the object of his praise. Instead of tears in the night, David discovers, "His song will be with me in the night" (v. 8). Thus, by the end of the psalm, we find a complete change in his perspective, for, in the conclusion, he no longer sees the reason for his despair; instead, he discovers his reason for praise. But it was not the circumstances that changed, it was his perspective of God.

As struggles and trials unfold in our lives, they will affect all of us differently. For some, they will be a mere inconvenience; for others, they will be life-altering. But for all of us, they are an opportunity to redirect our focus onto God, to thirst for Him. When God becomes the object of our desires, we have hope and find security even amid turmoil. So, spend time today reflecting upon God and asking Him to reveal Himself to you throughout this circumstance.

Day 4
The Certainty of God's Love

Read Psalm 136

For his lovingkindness is everlasting. Psalm 136:1

Psalm 136 is a psalm that provides a snapshot overview of the history of Israel and all humanity. The psalm begins with a reminder of God's supremacy—that He is the only true God who reigns over the universe. Then the psalmist moves from the throne of heaven to God's creative work on earth. In a few verses, he recounts that God is the creator and the one who brought all things into existence, both in the heavens and on the earth, merely with a spoken word. But God not only demonstrated His power in creation, He also demonstrated it in the redemption of His people as He delivered them from their bondage. The work of God in the Exodus event was significant, for it served to provide a picture of God's redemptive work in Christ when Christ brought the hope of salvation to all those who were captured by sin. But then the psalmist brings us to the despair of God's discipline and judgment, such as when He brought His severe punishment upon the nations of Canaan, as well as upon Israel when they rebelled against Him. Because they refused to trust in God's word, Israel wandered in the wilderness for forty years. However, the discipline of God did not mean He abandoned His people. On the contrary, when things looked the darkest for Israel, God again brought deliverance and rescued them from their adversaries.

This psalm is not just about the history of Israel, nor about the history of the people of earth through all their ups and downs. For there is a phrase constantly repeated like the steady pounding of a drum. It serves to shift our focus away from the uncertain course of life's experiences to the one thing remaining constant through all things. The phrase, "His loving-kindness is everlasting," repeated with each verse, provides an anthem of celebration of the loving-kindness of God. When we think of love, we think of it in terms of an emotional response. But the love spoken of here is more profound and enriched with meaning. The word points to the commitment God has to His people in the covenants He makes with them. It is a commitment in which He affirms in His fidelity to His people even with they demonstrate disloyalty to Him. It is a love that is not static but active. It is a love that moves God to action because He has pledged His unconditional love to us even when we are not deserving of it. It is this love that remains constant through all the upheaval of life, through times of deliverance, times of God's discipline, and times of uncertainty. In times of insecurity in our life, there is one thing that remains constant: God's deep, abiding commitment to His loyalty to us because of the covenant He made through the work of Christ on the cross. For the psalmist, this becomes the basis of his joy and gratitude.

Today, spend time just expressing your gratitude to God for His loving-kindness, which is neither fickle, nor temporary, nor conditional. Rather, it is eternal. When you start feeling the strain of the day, remember that His loving-kindness is everlasting.

Day 5
Rather than Asking Why, Ask Who

Read Job 1:13–22, 38:1–7

I know that You can do all things, and that no purpose of Yours can be thwarted. Job 42:2

In a few hours, Job's world was completely turned upside down. In dramatic and tragic fashion, he lost all his possessions and the thing most precious to him—his children. We can only imagine the depth of his pain as he was haunted by the question of *why*. Throughout the book of Job, we see Job and his friends wrestle with this question: Why do people suffer and experience tragedy? Yet even as Job laments his sorrow and wrestles with gaining some understanding of the events that befell him— even to the point of questioning the workings of God—his faith remains steadfast. From the outset, he affirms his trust in God, stating, "The LORD gave, and the LORD has taken away. Blessed be the name of the LORD" (Job 1:21).

However, his faith does not prevent him from questioning God's activities. In the subsequent arguments with his friends, each of them attempts to answer why Job is suffering. For Job, the answer seems to be hidden behind a reality that points to God being unjust. For his friends Eliphaz, Bildad, and Zophar, it is because of Job's sin. But ultimately, contrary to the traditional understanding that wisdom came from the aged, it is his youngest friend who points Job in the right direction.

Elihu arrives silently upon the scene and, for a time, sits and listens to the debate of those sitting on the ash heap of despair. Finally, he can remain silent no longer. Instead of arguing about Job's innocence or guilt, Elihu points them in a different direction. Instead of focusing on why people suffer, Elihu instead directs them to God, who is just in His dealing and remains sovereign over the affairs of men. Thus, Elihu opens the door for God to speak, beginning in chapters 37–41. Instead of answering Job's questions, God now redirects Job's thoughts to the question of *who*. Who is the one controlling the universe and governing all aspects of creation's existence? God!

Ultimately, God is not accountable to us; we merely submit to Him and trust in Him regardless of the circumstances. The ultimate question then is not "Why do I suffer?" but "Who is the one who controls and sustains the universe?" He is God, and that is sufficient. In these times of uncertainty, it is easy to be caught up asking why these things are happening, but we need to redirect our focus to the "Who." When we understand the greatness of God, the question "Why" is no longer critical. The only important truth is that we have a God who is still in control of the universe, the world, and our lives. After God's rebuke, Job concludes, "I know that You can do all things and that no purpose of Yours can be thwarted" (Job 42:2). For the child of God, that is all we need to know. We can never fully answer the question of why, but we can fully trust in the Who.

The Power of God

By the Word of the Lord the heavens were made, and
by the breath of His mouth all their hosts.
Psalm 33:6

The first thing that strikes us in times of trials and suffering is our impotence. In Mark 9:14–19, we find the story of a man who was at the end of his rope. He had come to the disciples looking for hope and found none. From birth, his son had been tormented by an evil spirit, leaving the father desperate. For years, this father had lived with the anguish of seeing his son not only plagued by this evil spirit, but also facing the scorn of people. After coming to the disciples and finding them powerless to help, his faith wavered as hope diminished. For him, even God seemed unable to help.

This sense of powerlessness is where suffering and trials lead us. Adversity confronts us with our frailties and reminds us that we are faced with circumstances that only highlight our weaknesses in the end. One such event was felt by the world when the COVID-19 pandemic swept across the globe. For all our technology, a virus invisible to the eye completely paralyzed our country, shook our economy, and gripped the world with fear. The same is true in the trials we face on a personal level. An unseen, microscopic cancer cell brings our world to a stop, as it confronts us with our mortality. In a moment, we can lose all the financial security we spent years trying to establish.

The real issue in Mark 9 was not the power of a demon, but the weakness of the faith of the father and the disciples. When the disciples sought to cast the demon out with their own strength, they failed miserably. Losing hope, the father then brought his son to Jesus, pleading for His help. Yet, in his request, we see the struggle of his faith. "If you can do anything," was his plea. This plea is from one who has realized his complete inability to handle the events he is facing. After years of looking for God to act, he began to question if God indeed had the power to help.

In response to his request, Christ brings him, and us, back to the center of our understanding of God. He reminds us that all things are possible with God (Matthew 19:26) because God is, in fact, omnipotent—that is, He possesses infinite power. However, His power is not raw, untamed power. When we speak of the power of God, it refers to His ability and capacity to do all that He wills in a way consistent with His nature. He can fulfill His purposes, both in the universe and in our lives, no matter how insurmountable the obstacles might be. Throughout Scripture, God is referred to as God Almighty (*El Shaddai*). This divine name or title for God is used forty-eight times in the Old Testament. This serves to highlight that God can control everything, and no one exceeds His power. No circumstances exceed His ability to control and command events to fulfill His purpose. When we go through trials, we are confronted with our inabilities and made to feel powerless. Yet, in the expression of God's power, we are reminded that no matter how out-of-control events may appear from our perspective, God always remains in command. The wavering of the father's faith in Mark 9 is what makes his response to Christ's comment relevant to us. When he states, "I do believe; help my unbelief" (Mark 9:24), he confesses that Christ not only has the power to do what is needed on behalf of his son, but also that Christ can transform his weak faith.

When we struggle with our faith in times of adversity, we can still rest in God, who gives us the confidence to trust in Him. Because He is both all-powerful and all-loving, we have assurance that He can act and is willing to work on our behalf. Thus, our security in life is no more threatened when we are going through adversity than when we are going through times of prosperity. We have the assurance that God's will and purpose for us are never frustrated by anything, anyone, or any circumstance. The bridge between His power and our serenity is faith. Our faith finds expression when we realize our inadequacy so that we are driven to prayer. In prayerful dependency, we discover the peace that comes from knowing that His power is at work in our lives and that every event, good and bad, is part of the outworking of His plan, which cannot be thwarted and is ultimately governed by His love.

Day 1
The Power of God: The Creative Power of God

Read Psalm 8

When I consider Your heavens, the work of Your fingers . . . what is man that You take thought of him? Psalm 8:3

An enjoyable hobby is night photography—capturing the Milky Way as it spans the heavens. One of the reasons it is enjoyable is that the camera captures the light and stars that our human eye cannot. While we can see a brush of the Milky Way's haze, we cannot know the magnitude of the stars and the details of the galactic center as it rises above the horizon. We marvel at the Milky Way because it reminds us of the infinite smallness of humanity in the face of such infinity. The lens gives us a glimpse into the millions of stars that compose the Milky Way. If you look closely enough, you can even see the oval shape of the nearest galaxy, the Andromeda Galaxy, which is a mere 2.5 million light-years away. So, when we investigate the heavens, we not only see the stars, but we also see a glimpse of creation itself.

David also felt our experience of awe in the face of such expanse. One can imagine David sitting on a rock at night, out in the pastures, as he carefully guarded the flock of his father, contemplating the wonder of heaven and creation itself. Then, in a thrilling awareness of God's creative power, David raises his anthem of praise to the Creator, "How majestic is Your name in all the earth who have displayed Your splendor above the Heavens!" (Psalm 8:1). He stands in awe of God of the omnipotent God who displayed such creative power merely with the work of His fingers. For David, all the wonders and expanse of the heavens were simply the fingerplay of God. So great is the power of God compared to the universe that Isaiah states that the vastness of the universe could fit in the palm of God (Isaiah 40:12). What an incredible and mighty God. While the universe reduces humanity to an infinitely minute speck of sand, God reduces the universe to a ball to be held in His hand!

Having been given a glimpse into God's infinite power, David is stunned that such a powerful God would show special attention to us. But even more wonderous than God's attention riveted upon us is the fact that He imprinted His image within us. What value, worth, and dignity He has bestowed upon each of us, from the smallest baby in the womb of a mother to the broken elderly on the doorstep of death, to each individual between them. It is a reminder that we have the almighty, omnipotent, and creative God watching over us amid all the events around us. So today, instead of becoming apprehensive in the circumstances surrounding you, marvel at the majestic glory of an all-powerful God who envelops you with His care.

Day 2
The Power of God: The Sustaining Power of Christ

Read Colossians 1:15–20

He is before all things, and in Him all things hold together. Colossians 1:17

What sustains us when our world seems to be falling apart? What hope do we have when life becomes broken, chaotic, and disintegrating around us? It seems to us today we face threats to our existence on a global level: COVID-19, global warming, nuclear war, terrorism, poverty, just to name a few. We also face threats to our well-being: economic collapse, the loss of a job, illness and death, crime, and the list goes on. These are real issues and life-altering events. So, in a world of insecurity and threats, where can we turn for security?

In Colossians 1:15–20, Paul gives us a kaleidoscope view of the person and work of Christ. Beginning with His deity and pre-eminence, Paul reminds us that Christ is not a mere man who was a wise religious teacher. He is the visible expression of the invisible God. He is God Himself who became flesh for us to see, hold, identify with, and follow. He is the creator of the universe and all humanity. Creation was not the work of random chance but the activity of an infinitely powerful and wise triune God. The Father formed the universe through the person of Christ and created all things for Christ. Thus, Christ not only stands at the beginning of creation as the one preeminent and the source of all life, but He also stands at the end of creation as the goal of all creation and history. He also is involved in the "in-between," for He is the one who brings salvation to people, and through Him, we are reconciled back to the Father.

In verse 17, we find the hope and answer for all the threats to our existence. Paul states that in Him, all things hold together as He keeps all the individual parts of creation functioning together as a whole. What sustains the universe is not indifferent laws of physics; it is not some philosophical ideal, but a person: Christ Himself. The planets move through space in predictable order; the weather continues to bring water to our world, the cells in our body continue to function all because of the power and person of Christ. This gives us confidence when it seems that the world is falling apart (both globally and personally). When we trust in chance, physics, or even human wisdom, the result will only bring fear, for what happens when they fail? We have confidence and hope when we recognize that we have an eternal, infinitely wise and powerful God sustaining us. When it seems as if our own personal world is falling apart because of circumstances beyond our control, we have confidence that no event ever threatens the One who sustains our world and our individual lives. When life seems out of control, remember there is one who is still in control and who has the power to support you in the darkest of times if you just trust in Him. When your faith is riveted upon Him, He puts the broken pieces back together and brings order and purpose back to your life. In Him, fear is replaced by faith.

Day 3
The Power of God: The Transforming Power of God

Read Romans 7:14–25

Who will set me free from the body of this death?
Romans 7:24

It is easy to put on a face of confidence and assurance that everything will turn out alright in times such as these. But often, such outward displays mask the inward anxiety and distress we are actually experiencing. It is easy to change the outward appearance, but it is far more challenging to alter our inward heart condition.

Paul understood the challenge we face. After expounding on the greatness of God's redemptive work in history through the first six chapters of Romans, Paul brings it home to himself by carefully and honestly assessing his own heart condition. What he finds disturbs him and leaves him with a sense of helplessness. Having seen the effects and control of sin in his own life, he concludes with an honest assessment, one that we easily resonate with: "For what I am doing, I do not understand; for I am not practicing what I would like to do, but I am doing the very thing I hate" (v. 15). He concludes, "For the willing is present in me, but the doing of the good is not." (v. 18). In our times of fear, anxiety, and apprehension, how do we change our inner thoughts, emotions, and attitudes? We desire to do what is right, but often we do the very thing we regret and despise. We want to be cheerful and encouraging to our family during stress but find ourselves responding with anger and frustration. We want to trust God's provision and rest in His promises but struggle with doubt and apprehension in times of uncertainty. We identify with Paul when he cries out, "Wretched man that I am! Who will set me free from the body of this death?" (v. 24).

Paul does not leave us hanging in the frustration of our weaknesses. Instead, he provides the answer, "Thanks be to God through Christ Jesus, our Lord!" (v. 25). In the subsequent chapter (chapter 8), he sets forth one of the greatest songs of God's victory and love, which gives us confidence in the most difficult of times. For Paul, the answer to his inward battles is not found in himself, but rather in the redemptive power of Christ. We are reminded of our inability to truly change our circumstances and the impossibility of changing our inward struggle with our attitudes and actions in these difficult days. But the power of God is superior. When we stop trying to save or change ourselves and instead learn to surrender to God's work, we find true freedom and victory, not only from our fears but from our struggles with inward attitudes and outward actions. Only when we trust in God and seek His help, do we find real victory over sin. When you find yourself apprehensive because of your circumstances and responding wrongly to others, ask God to give you the strength to change. He is powerful enough to do the one thing that is most difficult for you to do: change yourself.

Day 4
The Power of God: The Empowering Power of God

Read 2 Corinthians 12:7–10

My grace is sufficient for you, for power is perfected in weakness. 2 Corinthians 12:9

Paul desired relief. For some time, he experienced a debilitating weakness that he felt was destructive in his life and hindered his ministry. As a result, three times, he pleaded (a word implying more than a simple request but an earnest plea for help) for God to act and bring relief. What this "thorn in the flesh" was, we can only surmise. In his letter to the church at Corinth, he mentions several struggles he faced. Chapter 7 mentions several difficult circumstances that beset him: external conflicts, internal fears, depression, and physical exhaustion. In Galatians 4:13, Paul alludes to his struggle with physical illness, which some have suggested may have been a chronic disease such as malaria or epilepsy. Others have suggested that it was due to his extremely poor eyesight (see Galatians 4:15 and 6:11), which may have resulted from the beatings he received or some eye disease. On the other hand, it may have been from some demonic spirit oppressing him. Whatever it was, Paul was so profoundly affected by it that he begged God for relief.

However, God's response was as surprising to Paul as it is to us. Instead of answering his prayer in the affirmative and removing the obstacle, God gave him a resounding NO! But God's response was not because He was uncaring or indifferent. Instead, it stemmed from God's desire to do something even more remarkable than merely relieving Paul of his adversity. God desired to use Paul's experience to transform him eternally and give him a greater understanding of God and His purpose. By God saying no, Paul learned an even greater lesson, that God's power is at work in his weakness, empowering him to serve God in a more significant way than Paul could ever imagine. So often, when we are going through times of difficulty, we desire relief. We pray for God to remove the circumstances causing us anxiety and discomfort.

Nevertheless, in God's program, suffering is not a destroyer but a springboard to eternal transformation. At times, God does not alleviate our suffering because He recognizes that in our struggle, we learn to rely upon Him and rest in His eternal plan (Romans 5:3–5). In trials, not at ease, we genuinely understand the extent of God's love for us (Romans 5:5).

Through our suffering, we become better equipped to encourage others in their struggles (2 Corinthians 1:3–7). As a result, Paul states that he will glory in his weakness, for it is by the daily challenges that we learn the surpassing greatness of God's sustaining power. This becomes the paradox of faith: the weaker we become, the stronger we become. In our weakness, we learn to no longer rely upon our strength and abilities but upon God's empowerment. Although we do not know what the future holds (and for some of us, it may involve some deep waters of affliction), we do know God will not abandon or forsake us. Instead, as we learn to trust in Him more deeply, His infinite power will be present to sustain us through these times. A far greater threat to our spiritual health is the disease of self-sufficiency. Suffering provides the opportunity and cure for this disease, leading us to the genuine source of our strength: complete and total reliance upon God. If we learn this lesson, then, in the end, we will confess with Paul, "Most gladly, therefore, I will rather boast about my weaknesses, so that the power of Christ may dwell in me." Instead of just praying for deliverance, pray that God will use the experience to teach you to trust in His power.

Day 5
The Power of God: The Power of God's Protection

Read Deuteronomy 31:1–8

Be strong and courageous; do not be afraid or tremble at them, for the LORD, your God is the one who goes with you. He will not fail you or forsake you. Deuteronomy 31:6

Israel was now standing on the threshold of the promised land. After their initial failure to trust in God forty years earlier, they had spent the last four decades wandering in the wilderness in the southern Sinai and in what is today Jordan. God severely disciplined them because they feared the Canaanites more than they trusted God and refused to possess the land. After a new generation arose, they were ready to enter into the land promised them by God. Shockingly, the man who had led them faithfully and powerfully from the bondage of Egypt, through the forty years in the wilderness to the point of entry into the land, was not going with them. Because of his act of unbelief and disobedience, Moses was not permitted to enter the promised land. In Deuteronomy 31, we find Moses's final address to Israel before he passed the baton of leadership to Joshua. Because of the events unfolding, it is understandable that the people would be apprehensive. They were facing several military battles that would be their greatest challenge as a young nation. They were also confronted with the uncertainty of a change of national leadership.

In the face of such a challenge, Moses reminded the people that their leader was not Joshua but God Himself. In verse 3, Moses encourages the people that God Himself will go before them and prepare the way: "It is the Lord your God who will cross ahead of you." God is not merely standing behind them to shout encouragement to them, like a spectator at a sporting event. Instead, He advances in front, preparing the way for them. God will not let them down, nor will He abandon them in the lurch. When things get the toughest, God's presence and power become most evident. The same is true for us today. He remains faithful to His promise never to leave us or abandon us. When we face dire circumstances, God does not just position Himself behind us, or even alongside us. Instead, He places Himself in front, between us and the danger we face, to protect us with the might of His power.

Because of God's protective power, we can be strong and courageous. The term "strong" means to be powerful beyond the average or expected. The word "courageous" has the idea of facing and dealing with danger or fear without flinching. Because of God's power, we can have confidence that stands the test. We do not need to be hesitant or flinching in the face of the battle, not because we possess some inner strength or confidence, but because we have a God who is infinite in His power, positioning Himself in front of us, protecting and watching over us. So today, remember that God stands between you and the adversity you face. He will protect you and fight the battles for you. Only one question remains: will you and I will stand firm in our faith in Him or flee in fear because of doubt?

The Knowledge of God

You scrutinize my path and my lying down and are
intimately acquainted with all my ways.
Psalm 139:3

As humans, we are on an endless quest for knowledge. Whether it be the search to discover the laws governing the universe or the quest to find the foundations of the essential components of life itself, the more we ascertain in our pursuit, the greater our realization that we know very little. Yet, even more perplexing than the sciences is the quest for meaning and understanding of our existence. We struggle to understand why things happen in our life. We strive to discover purpose and meaning when life seems to be ruled by chance and confusion. It is no wonder that the quest for knowledge becomes a pursuit of the wind. Instead of expertise bringing joy, it leads us to a sense of futility and frustration. In the words of the sage in Ecclesiastes, it becomes utterly meaningless, and the more knowledge we gain, the more grief and sorrow it brings (Ecclesiastes 1:17–18).

In the pages of Scripture, in stark contrast to our finite and limited understanding, we discover that God is infinite in His knowledge. Romans 11:33–36 captures the depth of God's knowledge when Paul writes, "Oh, the depth of the riches both of the wisdom and knowledge of God! How unsearchable are

His judgments and unfathomable His ways." When we speak of God's knowledge, theologians have used the word "omniscience," which comes from the Latin phrase *omnis* (meaning all) and *scientia* (meaning knowledge), thus affirming that God knows all things. However, this knowledge means far more than a thorough understanding of all things in the universe. When we speak of the knowledge of God, we must go back in time, not just to the beginning of time but even beyond time itself. When we talk of God's knowledge, we refer to the fact that God knows all things from eternity past. There is nothing that will happen in the future that He has not already known in the past. Not only does He know all things actual, but He also knows all things possible: all possible options, and every possible outcome.

It has been estimated that the average person faces 35,000 choices each day, and often those choices that seem to be insignificant at the time can have life-altering effects. Sometimes a choice we make on a whim, without any conscious thought, has radical and life-altering consequences that we never anticipated. However, this is not the case with God. God knows all options of every choice and every outcome of every option. Therefore, He does not need a counselor, for there is no one who can add to or give further enlightenment to what God already knows, as Paul affirms: "For who has known the mind of the Lord, or who became His counselor?" (Romans 11:34). Because God knows all things, He never makes a mistake in what He does or His decisions. His actions are always perfect. It is no wonder that Paul cries out that God's judgments and ways are unfathomable and impossible to trace out.

God's knowledge is not abstract and impersonal. It is not cold and indifferent. Instead, it is personal and directed toward us. As we discover in Psalm 139, God knows every detail of our life and every thought we think. He knows every activity we do and every word we speak. As a result of His knowledge of us, the psalmist declares, "You (God) enclosed me behind and before and laid your hand upon me" (v. 5). The picture of the enclosure is that God has besieged him, which is often describing the work of an enemy who besieges someone so that no one can escape. Yet here, the picture is positive. He has surrounded us to watch over us because of His knowledge of us, and His hand has enveloped us with His care. The mighty hand of God, the one that measures the universe with a span, has now been placed as a protective shield over us.

How often in our finite understanding do we presume to judge God for what He does? How often do we bring God down to our level and think that somehow God should conform to our thinking? Too often, we reject the teaching of the Bible when it does not fit our understanding. As we face adversity, our struggles lead to confusion. We wonder if God knows what is happening in our lives and if there any purpose for the events. Yet, we can be confident in His infinite knowledge because He knows all things possible, and all possible outcomes. With this knowledge, God is guiding the events of your life for His purpose, a purpose that is good and right (Romans 8:28). This week, as you attempt to gain a glimpse into the infinite knowledge of God, give thanks to God, for He knows the outcome even when you do not.

Day 1
The Knowledge of a Caring God

Read Isaiah 46:1–13

I am God, and there is no one like Me, declaring the end from the beginning. Isaiah 46:9-10

"Hindsight is always 20/20." We use this expression to capture the frustration of having greater clarity and understanding after events come to pass than we had when choices were made. How often have we experienced the exasperation of looking back and wishing we could change the decisions we thought were correct at the time but only proved to be faulty in the end? Sometimes life would be much easier if we just knew the future. It would undoubtedly bring clarity to our decisions in the present.

In Isaiah 46:9–10, God distinguishes Himself from the pagan idols who are powerless and inept. In verses 5–7, God points out the folly of worshiping false gods who are made by man and must be carried from place to place, powerless to take care of themselves, much less provide for the people worshiping them. Nevertheless, idolatry is not just a practice in ancient days; it still plagues us now. Today, the idol is not a golden form created by man. Today, the idol has become a man himself. Instead of looking to God for moral clarity, we look to popular culture and opinion. When the teachings of Scripture conflict without our sensibilities, we casually cast aside the instruction of the Bible to follow the views of humanity. We label the Bible as archaic and misguided and humanity as enlightened. Secularism has become the new god. Yet, for all our "knowledge," we still do not know the future. We cannot guarantee that the moral path we have chosen is right because we do not know its outcome. Like the idols of ancient Canaan, we follow a modern god that, in the end, brings no guarantee of deliverance, protection, or guidance.

Standing in contrast to these gods is the God revealed both in Scripture and in the person of Christ. He knows not only all things past and present; He knows the future as well. From the very beginning, He knows the outcome. Before He created the world and He knew every event and the outcomes these events would bring about. Furthermore, He knows the result and guides all affairs to accomplish His ultimate purpose: to restore people to fellowship with Him. This brings us both comfort and a warning.

In verses 3–4, He provides us the comfort of His providential care. From the moment of conception until the last breath of our lives, He will care for us and guide us. Yet, there is also a warning that if we refuse to follow Him, we will reap the disaster of the destructive path we chose.

As the stock market staggers and events seem confusing, we can trust in a God who already knows the outcome. If we are willing to listen to Him and live by His Word, we can have the assurance that His knowledge will guide and protect us as we navigate these treacherous waters. So today, seek advice and direction from God, who already knows the outcome and has revealed His will in His Word. Surrender your life and future to Him, for He already knows what the end will be.

Day 2
The Knowledge of God: The Ignorance of Man

Read Isaiah 55:6–13

For as the heavens are higher than the earth, so are My ways higher than your ways and My thoughts than your thoughts. Isaiah 55:9

When we do not understand what God is doing, why He is doing what He does, or the aftermath, it is easy to begin to question God. We doubt God's knowledge of us when heaven remains silent in the face of our struggles. We are skeptical of God's understanding when His actions and commands seem to contradict our understanding of morality and fairness. We wonder about God's concern when adversity strikes. We distrust God's plan for us when things seem to go awry in our life. Sometimes we even question God's forgiveness when our past is filled with unspeakable failures.

In verses 6–7, Isaiah calls upon Israel to return to God and forsake their sin, for God will forgive and pardon them abundantly. Following this plea for Israel to turn from sin, verses 8–9 seem out of place. Why would Isaiah point to the contrast between God's thoughts and ours when he speaks of sin and forgiveness? One would have expected him to compare our righteousness (or lack thereof) with God's holiness and righteous standard. Instead, he points to our thoughts compared with God's thoughts. So why the shift? The answer lies in verse 7: "Let the wicked forsake his way, and the unrighteous man his thoughts."

Sin begins in our thoughts. Often, we do not choose evil because we want to sin; we choose to sin because it seems fitting to us. Adam and Eve ate the forbidden fruit in the garden because they thought it would bring them greater insight. To them, it seemed like the right thing to do. The sin of Adam and Eve was not just their rebellion against God's command but also the questioning of the truthfulness of God's decrees.

Isaiah contrasts our thoughts and God's thoughts. In a fallen world where our thoughts are corrupted by sin, what we think is right or wrong comes in conflict with what God says in His Word. Thus, the corrective set forth by Isaiah. When our understanding seems to conflict with God's understanding, we need to recognize who has more excellent knowledge. God's wisdom is infinite, encompassing all things actual and possible. He knows all options and every outcome of every choice. Our understanding, however, is finite and limited merely to the realm of our own experience. Therefore, it would be foolish for us to question God's wisdom and knowledge when it conflicts with ours. Instead, we must recognize the certainty of His Word (vv. 10–11). Verse 12 gives us a promise that we grasp and hold on to dearly: "For you will go out with joy and be led forth with peace."

But that promise is only valid when we have embraced the limits of our knowledge and trust solely upon the knowledge of God revealed in His Word.

In these times of uncertainty, when we are unsure what to do and what is right or wrong, we need to trust the only one who knows everything. The most important question is not, "What do we know?" but instead, it is, "Whom do we trust to know?" That is why we must be turning to the pages of Scripture for answers to all of life's most profound questions. Start spending time each day reading the Bible to gain the truth that only God can give. Then, conform your thoughts to God's, rather than conforming His thoughts to yours.

Day 3
The Infinite Knowledge of God

Read Psalm 147:1–6

He counts the number of the stars: He gives names to all of them. . . . His understanding is infinite.
Psalm 147:4

When we look at the stars, we realize our minuteness. When we start to count the stars, we are soon lost in the realm of the immeasurable. It is estimated that the stars in the Milky Way exceed one hundred billion. To grasp this number, if you were to count them out loud (one, two, three, four . . .), it is estimated that it would take 3,100 years, counting twenty-four hours a day. However, that perspective seems infinitely insignificant when we start to move out further in space. It is estimated that the largest known galaxy (IC1101) has an estimated one hundred *trillion* stars. Furthermore, it is estimated that there are over two trillion galaxies just in our observable universe. Now we have moved from the incomprehensible to the inarticulable.

When the psalmist was gazing into heaven and contemplating the vastness of God's knowledge, he realized that God not only could count the number of stars but gives them individual names that He remembers. As he discovers the expanse of God's knowledge, it is no wonder that he states God's understanding is infinite. Like wrapping our thoughts around the vastness of the heavens, it boggles the mind to understand the depth of God's knowledge.

While this proclamation of the vastness of God's knowledge is sufficient to cause us to pause in wonder, what is even more astounding is the context in which the Psalm points this out. This statement is bracketed by God's care and concern for those who are brokenhearted and afflicted! This is our hope and confidence. The God who knows all things, whose knowledge is so vast that even the heavens cannot contain it, brings to bear all the resources of His understanding to help us in the depths of our struggles and pain. God does not leave us in our condition, but knows every option, every solution, every possible outcome, and He utilizes this vast knowledge to provide the answer to our most profound need.

This active knowledge is best realized in His response to our greatest need: the need to remedy the consequences of sin. He did not leave us in our state. Instead, He provided the best solution possible, one that seems absurd to the most outstanding intellect, for He chose to bring salvation through the sacrifice of His Son so that we might obtain salvation apart from any effort or work on our part. The only requirement is that we come to acknowledge our spiritual bankruptcy and accept by faith the offer of salvation He gives. However, the tragedy is that we neither see the need nor accept the solution in our finite understanding.

So, in our ignorance, we reject it as foolishness. Yet the God who counts the stars and calls them by name also knows the best way to attain our salvation from the millions of options and outcomes.

No matter what your need is, whether it be the need for salvation, deliverance, healing, or just the need for wisdom in dealing with daily life, you can turn to the God of the universe. He is infinite in His knowledge and is willing to bring that knowledge to bear in addressing your struggles and issues. This indeed is a song of praiseworthy to be sung.

Day 4
The Knowledge of God: When God Knows "Little"

Read Matthew 6:7–8, 15–34, 10:26–31

Your Father knows what you need before you ask Him. Matthew 6:8

How easily we forget. We forget the grocery list we were supposed to take. We fail to return a call. We forget a password used to access a website. Every day we are bombarded with little details and pieces of information that escape our notice and soon pass from our memory.

In Matthew, on three different occasions, Christ reminds His disciples of the extent of God's knowledge of our lives. So involved is He that there is not the smallest detail He neglects to notice. In Matthew 10:28–31, Christ comforts His anxious disciples. In doing so, He reminds them that God is so involved in His creation that He sees even the death of a single sparrow. Then Christ takes it a step further by reminding us that even the very hairs on our head are all numbered. God not only counts the stars in heaven, but He also counts the number of hairs we have. Christ points out that we are so valuable in the sight of God that He knows more about us than we know ourselves.

The second example of the extent of His knowledge is found in Matthew 6:32. Here again, Christ highlights God's intimate knowledge by comparing His concern with the birds of the air and the grass of the field with His understanding and regard for us. He knows what every creature needs, and He provides for them. If God does so for the most unimportant parts of creation, which are here today and gone tomorrow, how much more will He care for us whom He created in His image? God knows what we need and acts to provide for us.

We find the third example that God knows our requests even before we ask Him in Matthew 6:8. The point that Christ is making is that God knows what we need even before we do. God is never reactive to the concerns we have; instead, He is always proactive, responding to meet our needs before we even know it.

These three examples convey that God's knowledge of us is personal and complete and reaches the smallest detail. Christ brings home the same point in each of these statements: do not be fearful and gripped with anxiety. Four times in chapter 6, Christ says that we do not need to worry in light of God's intimate knowledge of out every need. In chapter 10, three times, He reminds us not to live in fear. The reason is that Christ always knows what is happening in our lives, and He is actively involved. Our security is not found in circumstances, government bailouts, the stock market, or even in ourselves and our abilities. Our safekeeping is found in God.

Consequently, we are not to allow our present struggles to cloud our eternal perspective. Instead of being anxious about our circumstances, we can be focused on serving Christ. When you find yourself becoming worried about the events of the day, remember God because He remembers you. He even knows the littlest things of your life.

Day 5
The Knowledge of God: When God Becomes "Forgetful"

Read Jeremiah 31:31–34; Hebrews 10:11–18

And their sins and their lawlessness deeds I will remember no more. Jeremiah 31:34

The hardest thing to forget is the failures we have made in the past. Those events and acts that we have done bring the most shame and regret. We can forget many things, but these we never do. Even though we hide them in the deepest recesses of our minds, they come back to haunt us in the night with the pain of guilt. We fear that these things will be exposed to others, so we shroud them in a cloud of protective isolation.

In Jeremiah 31:31–34, God promises a New Covenant with Israel, for Israel has done the unthinkable: they have broken the covenant they made with God and pursued the gods of the Canaanites. God likened their disloyalty to a wayward wife who had abandoned the love of her husband to pursue lovers in the dark. Yet, even when Israel abandoned God, God did not abandon them. Instead of rejecting them because of their failure, He promised to make a new covenant that would be radically different from the old, one that would bring complete and final transformation to Israel. Unlike the old covenant that Israel made with God on Mt. Sinai that focused upon external activities, this covenant would result in exhaustive, internal change. They would now know God completely.

It is this new covenant that we celebrate in the church when we celebrate Communion. When we affirm the words, "This cup is the new covenant in my blood" (1 Corinthians 11:25), we are testifying of the new covenant mentioned by Jeremiah. As the writer of Hebrews then points out, this covenant was substantially different. Unlike the old covenant, which was inaugurated with the sacrificial blood of an animal, this covenant was inaugurated with the sacrificial blood of Christ when He died on the cross. Consequently, this covenant is eternal and brings about the change of heart. In the new covenant context, we are then given the promise that God will no longer remember our sins. This forgiveness is complete because of His work on the cross, no longer needing any other offering or sacrifice (Hebrews 10:18).

God does not remember our sins anymore (Hebrews 10:17). This becomes the paradox in which the God who knows all things from eternity past "forgets." This does not mean "forget" in the sense that He no longer knows about our sin (that would be impossible), but that God "forgets" in the sense of never letting the knowledge of those sins affect how He relates to us. He no longer views us in the context of our sin, but rather in the context of our righteousness in Christ. God now makes us entirely new so that the past is no longer significant. Concerning the effects of Christ's death, Paul states, "If anyone is in Christ he is a new creature; the old things passed away; behold, new things have come" (2 Corinthians 5:17). This is what we remember on Good Friday and Easter. We celebrate the work Christ did in removing the effects of sin so that those things we did in the past, no matter how shameful, are no longer a part of our identity and relationship with Christ. They are removed and made irrelevant in our life.

If you have embraced Christ as your savior, the past is now "forgotten" by God. He no longer views it as significant in your relationship with Him. Therefore, you have freedom from guilt and shame because you can glory in the transformation of the new covenant. Easter is not a celebration of a bunny who only brings candy; it is a celebration of a Lamb who brings complete and final forgiveness.

The Wisdom of God

For [the farmer's] God instructs and teaches him properly.

Isaiah 28:26

It is one thing to possess knowledge; it is another to use knowledge for the best purpose and achieve the most excellent outcome. To lack knowledge is tragic, but to fail to use knowledge correctly brings devastating results. We can understand all the facts of the universe, but the failure to properly apply that information leads us down the road to our ruin. The same may be said of power. To possess all ability but to lack wisdom is utterly frightening, for it leads to the gross abuse of power. Today, the tragedy is that we are inundated with data and information, but we are bankrupt when it comes to wisdom. This is what makes our understanding of God's infinite wisdom crucial to our faith and confidence in all His activity. As we have already affirmed, God knows everything, both actual and potential, but such knowledge becomes meaningless and even evil without wisdom.

When we speak of wisdom, it is more than just an intellectual quality; it is more than just being intelligent or resourceful. In Scripture, understanding is both a mental quality as well as a moral quality. To be wise is to use knowledge to achieve the best goal and the highest moral purpose. The wisdom of God is interwoven with the infinite knowledge of God, for it speaks of His ability to use His understanding to achieve the best possible outcome—and of the understanding of the best possible way to achieve that outcome. His wisdom means there is no second-guessing with God. There is no need for an alternative plan. God never needs to change His purposes. Furthermore, because God is the only one who is truly wise (Romans 16:27), He sets the standard for all wisdom.

As we look about the created world, we see the evidence of His wisdom. In Psalm 104:24, we discover creation was not the arbitrary activity of a bored God who merely made the universe on a whim. In His creative activity, He had design and purpose for all things. Not only does this mean that He formed all things with structure and purpose, but He is also moving all creation toward a goal. Creation and history are not the product of chance, the outworking of coincidence, or evolutionary processes. They are the work of a wise God who establishes order and purpose with a predetermined goal.

Divine order and purpose are not only veritable of the universe; it is true of every person. In Psalm 139:16, we find that God has numbered our days. The focus here is not just that God has established the length of our life but that He has determined the purpose for our existence. God created us uniquely in our personalities and physical make-ups and the dignity of our lives. Our dispositions, our characteristics, our uniquenesses are not the product of blind luck governed by the chance formation of our DNA. God formed us in such a way that He might fulfill His purpose in us. This plan begins even within the womb as He develops us uniquely and with a goal. In Jeremiah 1:5, we read, "Before I formed you in the womb I knew you, and before you were born I consecrated you." This is true not only for the prophet Jeremiah but for each one of us. We often judge ourselves by others. We feel inferior to others who seem to have more talents and abilities. This is dispelled by the understanding of God's work in our life. He uniquely made us with all our capabilities, personalities, talents, and skills to be in the best position and to be best equipped to perform His plan for us. All people, both born and unborn, have dignity and value because He formed us with design.

God's wisdom is seen in our formation, and in every circumstance of life. Paul states in Romans 8:28, "And we know that God causes all things to work together for good to those who love God, to those who are called according to His purpose." In other words, all our circumstances, even adversity and tragedy, are orchestrated by God to achieve the goal that He has for us. In His infinite wisdom, God not only uses all circumstances we face, but He does so with a perfect design and goal. This becomes our comfort amid trials that God's wisdom is on display no matter how difficult life becomes. He not only has a perfect intention for our lives; He knows the ideal means to achieve that plan. This includes His ultimate intent to conform us to His Son.

Not only does He possess all wisdom, but He gives us wisdom as well. Just as God gives the wisdom to the farmer to plant and harvest his crop at the right time, so He will provide you with the understanding for dealing and responding correctly to the struggles you are facing in your life. He will guide you in His purpose and give you the insight to react and choose the best options to achieve the best good in the issues that confront you.

Day 1
The Excellence of God's Wisdom

Read 1 Corinthians 1:18–25

> *But the foolishness of God is wiser than men.* 1
> Corinthians 1:25

"Education without wisdom is dangerous and destructive." This saying has been proven repeatedly throughout our history. Humanity delved deep into the atom's function and power and created a powerful energy source, but also built a bomb capable of unimaginable destruction. Studying the effects and working of viruses can both bring new hope to deadly diseases and be used for biological warfare by terrorists. Knowledge, when wrongly applied, brings harmful results.

This is why wisdom is so important. Wisdom is the ability to take what we have learned and apply it correctly to the circumstances and problems confronting us. When we face struggles, it is one thing to obtain understanding; it is quite another to use it to achieve the best conclusion. Wisdom provides this key. Wisdom serves as the bridge between knowledge and proper ethical conduct. It helps to guide us by utilizing knowledge correctly to achieve what is best.

To understand wisdom, we must begin with God. In Romans 11:33, Paul praised God for not only His infinite knowledge but also His endless wisdom. Last week we examined the knowledge of God—that God knows all things, both actual and potential, identifying all options and outcomes. With God, there is no regret; there is no looking back and wishing He would have acted differently. Because He knows all things, God does not guess or hope things will turn out all right. He already knows the outcome will be perfect.

God's wisdom stands in stark contrast to our folly. We make decisions based upon our limited understanding and then hope that the outcome will be correct. But in the end, it is nothing more than an "educated guess." Not so with God. He actively applies His infinite knowledge with His wisdom so that the outcome is always right and morally perfect.

Yet, we often do not see events and circumstances the same as God, and when God's actions and outcomes do not fit the effects we anticipated or thought best, we begin to question God. However, this is to our folly and destruction. When the circumstances of life seem to be damaging, if we are trusting God, we can rest in the knowledge that the outcome of His activities will always be perfect and achieve greater good than our feeble minds could understand or predict. We must recognize that in the face of an infinitely wise God, our most extraordinary thoughts are foolish in comparison. Instead of questioning God or seeking to usurp God, we can calmly relax entirely in Him. When we are submitting to God's direction, we may not understand all the reasons why we are going through challenges and difficulties. Still, we can have peace in knowing that He already knows the best possible outcome, and the circumstances confronting us are the best way to achieve those purposes. "With the goodness of God to desire our highest welfare, the wisdom of God to plan it, and the power of God to achieve it, what do we lack? Surely, we are the most favored of all creatures."[2]

Day 2
God's Wisdom in Salvation

Read 1 Corinthians 1:26–31

God has chosen the foolish things of the world to shame the wise. 1 Corinthians 1: 27

---

2. A. W. Tozer, *The Knowledge of the Holy* (Harper One, 1961), 65.

From man's perspective, God's work and wisdom seem foolish, for He often uses the most unexpected and unlikely ways and people to accomplish His eternal purpose. He uses death as a way of bringing life. Trials strengthen faith and produce greater peace. He defines leadership as servanthood. He works through untrained and uneducated men to convey a message that would confound the greatest intellects throughout history. He calls upon sinful and broken Individuals to be the conveyers His message of salvation. He elevates the last and debases the first. To find ourselves, we must give up ourselves. All of this serves to display the depth of His wisdom.

The greatest demonstration of His wisdom is found in the display in the folly (from man's perspective) of the life and message of Christ. The idea truly is beyond our understanding: the God of the universe would pay for the sins He did not commit to save those who rebelled against Him. In this, God placed His wisdom on full display. Paul states that Christ became the wisdom of God to us. That is, in Christ and His salvation, we see the infinite wisdom of God, who saw this one way as the only perfect way to bring about our salvation. By dying for us, Christ made our salvation possible. Any other way, any other means of salvation that places even some of the responsibility upon us, would be destined for failure, for we would never be able to fulfill our requirements, no matter how small they might be. In the end, we would never achieve salvation. The only option was for God to do the complete work for us. And this is what He did! This becomes the basis for our hope and joy. God has done it all for us. What an incredible promise this is. That we can enjoy the mercy and grace of God regardless of our past, for Christ fully satisfied the justice of God.

When we are going through difficult times, it is easy to question God's wisdom and focus on the trials assaulting us. In the end, we become discouraged and anxious. Nevertheless, the wisdom of the gospel lifts our perspective higher. It reminds us of two all-encompassing truths. First, God's wisdom is always perfect, even when it might seem foolish to us. The gospel of Christ may appear as foolishness to the wisest, but it is brilliant in its simplicity, scope, and result. We can find comfort in the assurance of our salvation that is grounded in the work of Christ rather than our efforts. Second, it serves as a reminder that God's wisdom exceeds ours. Even when we do not understand why the events are happening, we have a God who is orchestrating the events in our lives to achieve His best purpose for us. In these days, rather than complain about what is happening, rejoice in what God is doing. Spend time thanking Him for His promise that He uses these events to achieve His perfect plan for you, a plan that begins with your salvation and ends with an eternity spent with Him.

Day 3
The Wisdom of God in Creation: The Personification of Wisdom

Read Proverbs 8:12–36

The LORD possessed me at the beginning of His way.
Proverbs 8:22

Michelangelo's masterpiece in the Sistine Chapel depicts creation as God reaches out His right hand to touch Adam's finger. What has intrigued art students is the wonder of the painting and the woman nestled under God's left hand. Some have speculated that it was Eve. Others have argued that it was Mary, the mother of Jesus. However, a third view, one adopted by many, is that the woman is neither Eve nor Mary, but Lady Wisdom, who is personified in Proverbs 8.

In chapter 8 of Proverbs, wisdom is pictured as a lady calling out into the streets for all to come and listen to her instruction. She stands in contrast to Madam Folly, who also calls in the streets as a boisterous harlot calling to men to come and delight in her, but who, in the end, only brings destruction upon those who listen. While Madam Folly seduces with flattery and pleasure, Lady Wisdom promises righteousness. However, the writer of Proverbs moves from their appeal to the eternality of wisdom. From the beginning, wisdom was present with God and was at God's side when He created the heavens and the earth. Thus, wisdom is seen as more than an inanimate object but as a participant through whom God created the universe. Ultimately, the picture of Lady Wisdom points forward to Christ Himself, who is not only a prophet, a priest, and a king, but also the manifestation of all wisdom. Just as Christ fulfilled the threefold offices highlighted in the Old Testament social structures, He was also the quintessential wise man.

The point then of Proverbs 8 is that the wisdom of God was present and integrated into all of God's creative work. It was not arbitrary when God created everything, like a young child forming figures out of clay. His work was the accomplishment of an infinitely wise God who integrated design and purpose into all that He did to accomplish His eternal plan. His wisdom is grounded in and leading to righteousness and justice, for it is upon these paths that wisdom walks (Proverbs 8:29). Wisdom (that is, God's divine purpose, which is the perfect application of infinite knowledge) is woven into every detail of God's activity, including in His design, purpose, and work in each of our individual lives. God has made each of us unique and brings different circumstances and events into our lives with purposefulness and design grounded in His goodness. We are not just a blob of mass from conception that forms into the likeness of humanity. From the very beginning of our existence, in the womb of our mothers (see Psalm 139:13; Jeremiah 1:5), God, with His infinite wisdom, designs our personalities and beings and then orchestrates the events of our lives to shape and direct us to a purpose that He desires for us as individuals. This ultimately culminates in the form of His image reflected in us.

The unfolding events of each day affect each of us differently. For some, trials are an inconvenience; for others, they are life changing. But this is precisely how God designed it. Adversity affects us differently because God has a different purpose for each one of us. Only an infinitely wise and powerful God could take one event shared by many and use it in a million different ways to affect each of us differently. No matter what tomorrow may bring, if you trust in Christ, you can know that He will use whatever happens for a perfect purpose in your life. So, instead of focusing on *what* is happening, trust in God to orchestrate *why* it is happening and the outcome it will achieve.

Day 4
The Wisdom of God's Individual Plan

Read Jeremiah 1:4–10

Before I formed you in the womb, I knew you, and before you were born, I consecrated you. Jeremiah 1:5

Little did Jeremiah realize the cost he would pay when God called him to be a prophet. We can imagine the thrill Jeremiah experienced when God spoke directly to him and called him to his particular ministry. At the time of this call, it is estimated that Jeremiah was between the ages of fifteen and twenty. However, the joy Jeremiah must have experienced was soon lost in the trials and struggles he faced in announcing judgment upon the nation of Israel for their sin. The opposition and persecution he would face resulted in bouts of emotional and spiritual depression as he struggled with understanding God's plan. Jeremiah would suffer imprisonment, rejection, and exile. On one occasion, he would be thrown into the bottom of a well, where he would sink deep into the mud and be left to starve to death (Jeremiah 38:6). In despair, he would accuse God of deception (Jeremiah 20:7) and, like Job, would curse the day he was born (Jeremiah 20:14). In the end, he would become known as the weeping prophet.

Yet throughout the whole ordeal, we are reminded that God knew him and equipped him from birth to accomplish His purpose. While the people of Jeremiah's day regarded him as a prophet who only announced terrible news, it would be through the lips of Jeremiah that God would proclaim the greatest hope of humanity. Through Jeremiah, the promise of a new covenant was given, a covenant that would promise Israel's complete and final restoration and the hope of all humanity (Jeremiah 31:31–37).

God's wisdom is not seen just in His work in creation but also in His activity in the lives of His people. Like Jeremiah, even before our birth, God is working and moving in our lives in such a way that His perfect purpose is accomplished. This does not mean that we are insulated from adversity. Adversity is often a part of His plan and is used by Him to bring us into conformity with His will so that the character of Christ will be fully reflected in us. God has a more excellent and wiser plan than just making us happy, for emotional happiness is ultimately temporary. God has a greater goal in mind. He desires to transform us into His image and equip and use us for His glory and our ultimate good. His perspective is eternal, culminating in the joy of heaven when we share in the Father's deep love for Christ. To accomplish this purpose, we must go through challenging circumstances that form and shape us to that end. Like a loving father who understands that the joy of learning to ride a bike far outweighs the pain, so God allows adversity to bring about the pleasure of knowing Him and sharing in the character and inheritance of Christ.

As we go through the various circumstances of life, we have the confidence and comfort that an infinitely wise God uses these events to bring us closer to Him and expand our ministry for Him. When we do not understand why God is allowing adversity in our life, we can trust Him that He is guiding us with His infinite wisdom to accomplish His goal for us. Today, thank Him for His perfect plan, and instead of focusing on the trials, focus on how you can reflect Him amid the struggle.

Day 5
The Wisdom of God and Our Search for Wisdom

Read Proverbs 1:1–8

The fear of the LORD *is the beginning of knowledge.*
Proverbs 1:7

Adversity, trials, and tragedy leave us with a sense of hopelessness and despair. We do not know what is happening; we simply do not know how to respond. Unfortunately, this is not just true of tragedy: it is also often true of life itself. Daily we are confronted with issues that perplex us and leave us lost in the search for how to respond. This is where the writer of Proverbs enters our world and seeks to provide answers. The book of Proverbs is meant to be a book that offers insight into life's practical affairs. It is a book that deals with the daily nitty and gritty of life.

In Proverbs, the wise person does not necessarily possess excellent intellect, wealth, or status. Instead, the prudent person lives within the moral order that God established in His creation. If the wisdom of God refers to God's understanding of the best possible goals and the best possible way to achieve that goal, then human discernment is living in conformity to God's orchestrated plan.

For the sage, the starting point for genuinely being wise is found in the fear of the Lord. Yet this is not just the starting point from which one starts the journey and then leaves behind, like a sprinter who leaves the starting blocks behind as he runs the course. Instead, the fear of the Lord is the central and guiding point. Like the North Star was to sailors in the night, so the fear of the Lord is the focal point providing direction at every step of the way. To lose sight of the fear of the Lord at any point in the journey is to abandon the path of wisdom. To fear the Lord is more than just a sense of awe and wonder before God or to fear God's punitive hand when we do wrong. The fear of the Lord is to commit oneself to know God, respond in obedience to God's Word, love Him and serve Him, and be utterly devoted to Him. To fear the Lord is to set Him as the highest priority of life.

This is what brings clarity in our days of confusion. When the storms assailed and the waves drove the ship off course, the wise sailors looked to the North Star as their anchor of direction. So, as we become lost in the emptiness of our present struggles, we are to look to God and His Word as the anchor point of life. Then we will have the wisdom to know how to respond to whatever life may throw at us. In our age, when we are being driven aimlessly by the confusing reports and directives, we can find our true north in the person and Word of God. The fool is not the one who lacks intelligence: it is the one who lives without the fear of the Lord as his focal point. In his inauguration address, Franklin

D. Roosevelt stated, "So, first of all, let me assert my firm belief that the only thing we have to fear is . . . fear itself—nameless, unreasoning, unjustified terror which paralyzes needed efforts to convert retreat into advance."[3] In reality, our greatest fear is that we would live without fear—the fear of God.

When you become anxious regarding the circumstances you face, do not start by looking at the news, experts, or the latest quip on Facebook. Instead, start by looking to God for wisdom. "But if any of you lacks wisdom, let him ask of God, who gives to all generously and without reproach, and it will be given to him" (James 1:5).

---

3. Franklin D. Roosevelt, *First Inaugural Address*, http://historymatters.gmu.edu /d/5057/, accessed 8/27/2021.

The Wisdom of God and Suffering

Who teaches us more than the beasts of the earth
and makes us wiser than the birds?
Job 35:11

When we are going through trials, it is easy to begin to question the wisdom of God. If wisdom can choose the best process to achieve the best outcome, how can that include suffering? However, this is not a new struggle; it is one we see in the Bible as people struggled to reconcile their experience with the plans and purposes of God. One such person was Jeremiah. The initial joy of his call to ministry soon became lost with the struggles he faced. In Jeremiah 20:7–8, we find him lamenting, "O LORD, You have deceived me, and I was deceived . . . for each time I speak, I cry aloud; I proclaim violence and destruction, because for me the word of the LORD has resulted in reproach and derision all day long." What Jeremiah thought would be a well-received ministry pronouncing blessing and joy turned into the proclamation of judgment and desolation, resulting in constant ridicule. We assume that our lives' outcomes will be pleasant when we strive to live in obedience to God. When they are not, we begin to question God.

Nevertheless, even as we struggle to understand, we see the answers our questions in Scripture. We often view events that happen in our life from a temporal perspective. We evaluate the circumstances in our life by the effect it has upon our present attitudes and actions. However, God looks at events from an eternal perspective—that is, how they will affect us eternally. We do not see, nor can we see, how God weaves the pain we experience into His permanent plan leading to our spiritual growth and the salvation of others. Yet, we are not left in the dark to aimlessly search for purpose or meaning behind the tragic events that seem to strike us without rhyme or reason. Instead, we find that God uses suffering to accomplish His goals in several ways, even amid our most difficult circumstances.

First, suffering accomplishes a redemptive purpose (Colossians 1:24; 2 Corinthians 4:8–12). God uses suffering as a means of showcasing our faith to others to reveal the reality of our salvation. In trials, our testimony establishes credibility to the world around us. Thus God works in our lives to provide an opportunity for Him to manifest His power and strength through us so that others might come to Him.

Second, suffering teaches us dependency upon Him (Philippians 4:10–13). It is easy to become self-sufficient. However, we habitually rely upon our intellects, skills, talents, and ability to navigate life. Sufferings and trials serve to remind us that we are ultimately powerless and must depend upon God.

Third, suffering reveals the genuineness of our faith (1 Peter 3:15). It is easy to maintain the façade of spirituality when things are going well, and there is nothing to challenge the depth of our faith. However, when adversity strikes, then what we believe will be revealed. Sometimes suffering is the avenue through which God bestows His blessing upon us. It gives voice to the expression of our faith, demonstrating to others that what we believe is not just a set of creeds we confess but a truth we embrace and live.

Fourth, suffering brings transformation (James 1:2–4). Suffering refines our faith. It is the tool God uses to develop our character. Frequently, we fail to recognize that God is more concerned about what He is doing in us than through us. As a parent, we realize that the most unloving thing to do is to insulate our children to the point where they do not experience any suffering or pain. The growth to maturity involves suffering, and attaining happiness involves pain at times. To learn the depth of love, we must be vulnerable to experience the pain of rejection. To understand the thrill of victory, we must go through the discomfort of training. The path of trials often attains success and growth.

Last, suffering equips us for ministry (2 Corinthians 1:3–4). God calls us to minister to broken people facing trials and difficulties. The most effective minister is not the one standing on the sidelines shouting trite and hollow words of encouragement. Instead, it is the one who has experienced the pain and sorrows others face, who knows firsthand their anguish. We learn how to help those facing similar trials to find strength in their faith through our suffering.

When confronted with turmoil and pain, we look for deliverance rather than perspective. While the Scriptures do not always promise us liberation, they bring clarity to our life problems. Through the pages of Scripture, we find the answer that enables us to be spiritually revived even in life's struggles. In life's difficulties, we learn to trust in God's wisdom. He knows the best way to accomplish the greatest good in our lives, which sometimes involves suffering.

Day 1
God Uses Suffering to Transform Us

Read Genesis 50:15–21

*You meant evil against me, but God meant it for good
to bring about this present result.* Genesis 50:20

Joseph's brothers were more than stricken by grief at their father's death; they were plagued by fear. Years earlier, in an act of jealous rage, they had sold Joseph to a band of Midianite traders who would take Joseph to Egypt and sell him as a slave to Potiphar (a senior administrator in Pharaoh's court). As a result, his life would be turned into a roller coaster of events: he would rise to prominence in Potiphar's household, be falsely accused, and languish for years in prison, only to be elevated to a position of authority (second only to Pharaoh himself in all of Egypt). Consequently, when Jacob died, Joseph's brother feared he would now use his power to enact revenge upon them. However, Joseph understood what the brothers had overlooked. God utilized all the circumstances in Joseph's life to accomplish the physical salvation of his family from famine and the spiritual transformation of his brothers. God used the experiences of Joseph to change them from a bunch of self-centered hooligans to men of faith worthy of being the forefathers of the twelve tribes of Israel.

Suffering is not arbitrary in God's program. God's sovereign wisdom works not only to protect believers from facing more than we can handle (1 Corinthians 10:13) but also to orchestrate those trials in such a way that they achieve His transformational purpose in our lives and in the lives of others. Furthermore, as we see in the case of Joseph, God's purpose in our lives cannot be thwarted even by others' destructive actions.

Shortly before his death in a Gestapo prison, Dietrich Bonhoeffer, one who understood the cost of following Christ and the personal pain it brings, wrote in his last letter to his fiancée before his execution, "Stifter once said, 'pain is a holy angel, who shows treasures to men [that] otherwise remain forever hidden; through him, men have become greater than through all the joys of the world.' It must be so, and I tell this to myself in my present position over and over again—the pain of longing which often can be felt even physically, must be there, and we shall not, and need not, talk it away. But it needs to be overcome every time, and thus there is an even holier angel than the one of pain, that is one of the joys in God."[4] Suffering is more than just something we must endure. It is the teacher that God uses to mold and shape you. Through the lesson of travail, you often learn the most about yourselves and the God you serve.

Day 2
God Uses Suffering for a Redemptive Purpose

Read Acts 16:22–34

They said, 'Believe in the Lord Jesus, and you will be saved . . . and immediately he was baptized, he and all his household.' Acts 16:31,33

Paul and Silas were in the one place where no one would want to be: in a dark, damp Roman prison, feet fastened in stocks, recovering from fresh wounds obtained by a brutal beating inflicted by the Romans. At first glance, it appeared the opposition had won. Instead of the people rejoicing because a young girl had been delivered from demonic possession, they had turned against Paul and Silas. As a result, Paul and Silas found themselves badly beaten and in prison.

Despite their circumstances, Paul and Silas revealed their complete trust in God through three astonishing acts. First,

---

4. Eric Metaxas, *Bonhoeffer* (Nashville: Thomas Nelson, 2010), 495.

instead of cringing in frustration and anger that God allowed such a thing to happen, they sang praises to God, trusting in His deliverance and using the opportunity to be a witness to others (v. 25). Second, as a Roman citizen, Paul could have relied upon his legal rights to insulate him from false arrest and beating. Why he did not mention his citizenship until the following day, we can only guess. Perhaps in the shock and upheaval of the events, Paul completely forgot to mention it (unlikely). Maybe Paul trusted that God had a greater purpose, and he would wait to see what it was (more probable). Whatever the reason for Paul's silence, Paul was not sitting in the throes of despair because of his circumstances. Instead, he trusted in God's sovereign work in his life and ministry. Third, even when God provided supernatural deliverance, offering them the opportunity to flee, they calmly waited, trusting that God had a greater purpose to achieve than just their escape (vv. 26–28).

While Paul and Silas did not have the opportunity to understand the purpose behind their distress, we have the privilege of seeing the result as we read the narrative. What must have seemed to them like a traumatic turn of events was actually God orchestrating the affair to provide an opportunity for Christ to be manifested through them in such a way that the jailor and his family would come to realize the grace and forgiveness of Christ (vv. 26–34).

In this story, we find a critical principle of God's wisdom operating in our suffering. We often view suffering to be a threat to our well-being and to God's purpose for our lives. However, what we view as a threat to God's work often provides an opportunity for God to manifest His power and strength through us as a testimony for others to see. God uses the trials we face as an opportunity for others to see the power of His gospel at work in us. Paul would later write to the church at Philippi, "For to you it has been granted for Christ's sake, not only to believe in Him, but also to suffer for His sake" (Philippians 1:29). As you are going through difficulties, instead of focusing upon the problems, focus on the opportunity to share your faith so that others might ask why you have hope in a time many feel hopeless.

Day 3
God Uses Suffering to Realign Our Perspective

Read 2 Corinthians 4:7–18

For momentary, light affliction is producing for us an eternal weight of glory. 2 Corinthians 4:17

It is easy to lose perspective. In our fast-paced lives, it is easy to get caught up in the drive to achieve success and economic prosperity and to chase the allure of materialism. In an age where our position and social status measure success, we can become so focused on accomplishments that we lose sight of the essential things. Relationships become secondary to our goals and plans. We substitute genuine and meaningful relationships with super-ficial and meaningless posts on Facebook and other social media forms. We carry around our cell phones so we won't miss a call, but never really connect with people in significant face-to-face interactions. We fill our days with activities while neglecting our relationships with people and our relationship with God. We are too busy to go to church, but not to go to a sporting event, a concert, or to watch the latest movie. We fear the tediousness of boredom more than the tyranny of the busy.

Paul understood suffering and trials. The litany of troubles he faced (see 2 Corinthians 11:23–29) would cause even the most courageous to be overwhelmed. He compares himself to a clay pot that is easily broken with the slightest pressure. However, instead of becoming discouraged and angry at these circumstances, or even at God, they served to as continual reminders to him of what is truly important. When Paul compared his troubles with the impact they had upon others' lives, it caused him to rejoice. Every day he saw himself being delivered continuously over to death. However, this only served to clarify his perspective that life is not measured by what we achieve in the present, but by what we accomplish for eternity. The suffering and trials of this life are temporary; however, the transformation of people into followers of Christ brings eternal rewards.

When we are going through times of difficulty, it is often God's tool to realign our perspective and focus on the things that are important rather than what we *think* is essential. What is vital is not the impressiveness of our portfolios, the status of our bank accounts, or the success of our ventures. What is important is our relationship with God, our connections with people, and our time interacting with our families. Trials and adversity are the tools God uses to strip away the insignificant in our life to help us see clearly what is truly meaningful. It is not what we accomplish in the present but what we accomplish for the eternal that matters. Wealth, success, recognition, and status are all temporary. What is eternal is the pursuit of the knowledge of Christ, the testimony we share with others, and the service we give to Christ in building His church. The greatest tragedy is not the loss of income or the loss of the things we enjoy; the greatest tragedy is when we fail to learn from the circumstances that God is using to realign our priorities. Ask yourself the following questions: What is essential in my life? Does the use of my time, energies, and resources reflect those priorities? What changes do I need to make in my life to become more focused on Christ and His ministry?

Day 4
Regaining Perspective amid Suffering

Read James 1:2–8; Psalm 119

If any of you lacks wisdom, let him ask of God. James
1:5

When we are going through trials, it is difficult for us to understand God's activity and how we are to respond appropriately
to the challenges we face. In response, James begins by calling
upon us to do the unthinkable, to rejoice in our suffering. Yet,
how can we rejoice in something that seems so harmful and tragic? This is what gives rise to James's appeal for us to ask God for
wisdom. The wisdom that he is searching for is the wisdom we
need when going through trials. While knowledge speaks of our
ability to determine right and wrong, wisdom allows us to utilize
our understanding correctly. This is what we need in times of
suffering.

This leads us to the psalmist. In our search to gain wisdom,
where do we turn? The psalmists were well versed in the pains of
life. Their honesty as they present their laments before God captures the feelings and pains we wrestle with ourselves. However,
the appeal of the Psalms stems from the unwavering confidence
the writers had in the response of God to their cries. Even during their most profound anguish, the psalmists express assurance that God will soon bring their deliverance (see, for example, Psalm 13). But we wrestle with the question, how could the
psalmists remain so confident in the face of so much hardship?
The answer lies in Psalm 119. When life pressed down upon the
psalmists to the point where their souls "[wept] because of grief"
(v. 28), rather than abandoning themselves to the pit of despair,

they turned to the pages of Scripture. Over and over again, the psalmist in Psalm 119 sees the Scriptures as the source of his comfort and revival:

My soul cleaves to the dust; revive me according to Your word. (v. 25)

My soul weeps because of grief; strengthen me according to Your word. (v. 28)

This is my comfort in my affliction that Your word has revived me. (v. 50)

If Your law had not been my delight, then I would have perished in my affliction. (v. 92)

I am exceedingly afflicted; revive me, O LORD, according to Your word. (v. 107)

As we devote ourselves to the study of God's Word, sometimes we overlook the comfort of His Word. When confronted with turmoil and pain, we look for deliverance rather than perspective. While the Scriptures do not always promise us relief, it brings clarity to the problems we face in life. Through the pages of Scripture, we find the answers that enable us to be spiritually revived even in the pain of ministry. When we discover this renewal, we are genuinely equipped to proclaim God's message to a broken world. In His Word, we find the wisdom we need to respond rightly to the struggles of the day.

Day 5
God Uses Suffering to Reveal the Genuineness of Our Faith

Read Job 1:1–22

*Through all this, Job did not sin, nor did he blame
God.* Job 1:22

Job had it all. He had wealth; he had recognition and respect;
he had a family that genuinely cared for one another. Yet, because Job had everything, he became the target of Satan's dia-
bolical plan to reveal the fickleness of his faith. In Satan's twisted
mind, Job was only obedient because God had richly blessed him.
However, God knew what Satan could never grasp: that true faith
is not driven by circumstances, it is driven by the transformation
of the heart. Thus, while Satan sought an opportunity to destroy
Job's faith, God used it as an opportunity to demonstrate an expression of true faith even in the face of unbelievable disaster.
Given free rein, Satan brought Job's world crashing down around
him in a rapid series of events. The only thing left for Job was
a wife whose sole counsel was to curse God and die, and four
friends, three of which joined in the assault by questioning Job's
character.

Genuine faith becomes most evident when circumstances
seem to point to the opposite—when the things we believe are
challenged and seem to be untrue. Songwriter Laura Story points
this out in her song "Blessings," a song written from the context of the pain of real-life trials and adversities, written when
her husband was diagnosed with a brain tumor. One of the many
questions the song asks is, "What if trials of this life, the rain, the
storms, the hardest nights are Your mercies in disguise?" Laura
points us to the answer by asking the question—that suffering is
often the avenue through which God bestows His blessings upon
us. Suffering is the voice that expresses our faith, revealing to
others that what we believe is not just a set of creeds we confess
but a truth that we embrace and live.

This was the case for Job. Even at the end of his life, Job did
not realize the impact his story would have—not only on his

contemporaries but on countless others who would go through their own "Job experience." In his narrative, we find hope that God remains faithful no matter what might assault our faith and that He will sustain us even when heaven seems silent. This becomes the power of our testimony. Peter reminds us in 1 Peter 3:13–15 that our faith becomes a radiant lighthouse for others to see and wonder about when we are going through trials. Like Job, the struggles we face become the spotlight God uses to highlight the genuineness of our faith so that by it, others might be strengthened. This, in turn, leads to their acceptance of the gospel as they seek the hope that we have. No one enjoys trials, but when we continue to demonstrate our faith, we know that the difficulties we face are not without an eternal purpose. It reveals and strengthens our faith and the faith of others, and in the end, that is what makes suffering a blessing. Today, ask God to give you a faith that is radiant and visible to others, both in times of blessing and in times of suffering.

The God Who Is Present

For where two or three have gathered in my name, I am there in their midst.
Matthew 18:20

W hen adversity strikes, we can quickly become overwhelmed with an awareness of isolation from people. Even when we are with a crowd of people, we are mindful that our sorrow and anxiety only adds to our sense of solitude. According to research, our country is facing an epidemic of loneliness. The Health Resources and Services Administration reports that two in five Americans sometimes or always feel they lack meaningful relationships. In addition, one in five say they feel lonely or socially isolated.[5] Researchers further warn that loneliness and social isolation can damage our health as much as smoking fifteen cigarettes a day.

In Psalm 139, David is overwhelmed with isolation and rejection. Yet, amid his sorrow, he finds renewed strength in the awareness of God's eternal presence. In so doing, he provides us a glimpse into the omnipresence (all-presentness) of God. In the Ancient Near East, the common belief was that the gods were localized deities whose influence was confined to a specific area.

---

5.   https://www.hrsa.gov/enews/past-issues/2019/january-17/loneliness-epidemic, accessed 8/27/2021.

Against the backdrop of such polytheism, David affirms that God is unlike all the other gods, for He is a God who is always present.

When we say that God is omnipresent, it means more than just that God is everywhere. It speaks of the fact that God does not have a size or spatial dimensions. Because He is not confined spatially, He is present with His whole being at every point of space. God is not limited by space as we are, for God is the one who created space (Isaiah 66:1–2). We cannot be in the past, present, and future at one time. However, God can.

Furthermore, when we speak of God being omnipresent, we refer to the fact that He can both be everywhere in His complete person at one time, and He is always present everywhere—past, present, and future. In our minds, we often think of God as distant, up in heaven awaiting our arrival. On the contrary, God is just as present with us now as He is present in heaven, where the angels sing His presence.

Not only is He present with us in every location, but He is also present with us in every situation we encounter at every moment. David provides the scope of His presence by putting forth two extremes. He speaks of heaven, which refers to the outer reaches of the universe. Then he refers to Hell, which is the lowest region of the universe, the place of deepest despair, where God seems completely absent. Yet, God's presence in both areas points to an important principle. God is no nearer to us when "we feel His nearness" than when He seems "far and distant." There are times when we sense the presence of God, when we are experiencing His blessing and see His activity in our life, and when prayer seems natural and powerful. There are also times when God seems absent, when heaven seems silent, and prayer seems pointless and useless. However, David reminds us that regardless of each experience, God is no nearer or farther. He is entirely present, unconfined by temporal and spatial limits, in every circumstance and corner of the universe.

It is in His eternal presence that we find comfort during our darkest times. Even when we feel most alone, we have the assurance that God is as present with us as He is present with the angels in heaven. We are never alone. He is not just present as a casual observer. He is present to provide care, guidance, and protection. He is present in our world and remains engaged in our situations, knowing every event that happens in our lives and every activity we do.

Day 1
The God Who Is Present: The Universal Presence of God

Read Jeremiah 23:16–24

'Do I not fill the heavens and the earth?' declares the LORD. Jeremiah 23:24

How do we wrap our minds around the incomprehensible? It is easier to understand God's character qualities when they correspond to what we see in ourselves. As individuals created in the image of God, many of His qualities are imprinted in our being (albeit as a shadow rather than the fullest expression). We have mental capacities that provide a glimpse into the knowledge and intellect of God. We know what it means to express love so we can have some inkling of God's love. But His omnipresence is impossible for us to understand. When we try to explain it, we become confronted with the difficulty of explaining something for which we have no starting point of reference. In Jeremiah 23:16–24, God confronts the false prophets who presume to speak for God. They reveal their corruption because they dare to preach a message contradicting the warnings of the judgment coming upon those who reject Him. While God pronounced the certainty of judgment, they came preaching a message of peace and tranquility even to those who scorned God. Like the modern preachers who denounce any reality of divine justice and judgment, they proclaimed that even the most rebellious did not need to fear God. Under the guise of possessing a prophetic mantle, they declared their "vision of their own imagination" (v. 16). They elevated themselves to the position of God by proclaiming their own message and divine authority. While doing so, they thought God would not notice.

In response, God reminds them of His omnipresence. God is not distant, living on some far-off heavenly throne, uncaring what goes on in this speck in space. Instead, He fills and inhabits the heavens and earth. When we speak of God's omnipresence, we are affirming two essential truths. First, God is wholly present everywhere without being confined to any one location. Second, God does not have a size or spatial dimensions, or limitations. He is present everywhere in His created universe, yet He is not confined to His created universe, and He is entirely distinct from creation. Thus, there is not one place in the universe where God is more present or less present.

The glimpse into His omnipresence is what brings us to the realm of wonder as well as caution. To stand in the presence of an infinite God is to stand in awe. It is not just that God is powerful enough to create the universe we see, but His being fills the universe—and beyond. Yet we often elevate ourselves in importance and think that we know more than God. Like the false prophets, we believe we can redefine what God has said—and that we can tell Him what He should do. It is folly to think that we, who fill only in the tiniest speck of space, can counsel a God who fills the universe.

On the next clear night, go outside and look at the stars. Not only do we see a glimpse of eternity, but we see a glimpse into the magnitude of God's being. Then bow in humble praise and thanksgiving and submission, for the God who cannot be contained in the universe is a God who is present with you every moment of your life, and a God who has spoken His Word to you for you to believe and follow without hesitation.

Day 2
The God Who Is Present: Sustaining the Universe

Read Colossians 1:15–20

He is before all things, and in Him, all things hold together. Colossians 1:17

The threats are real and seem never-ending. We face the threat of pandemics and diseases. We see the slow decay of the world around us. We are informed that humanity's very existence is threatened by global warming, massive famines, unparalleled storms, and unpredictable earthquakes. Facing these threats, people become fearful with a misguided notion that humanity must somehow save the planet even as we neglect to deal with the root cause of its decay—the reality of our rebellion against God.

While we are not to minimize the dangers, there is a greater hope than men's wisdom. Ultimately, it is God, not human effort and understanding, that sustains the universe. In Colossians 1, Paul highlights Christ's supremacy over creation (vv. 15–16). When he states that Christ is the firstborn of all creation, he is not referring to Christ being the first act of God's creative power, but that Christ stands in a position of preeminence over all creation. He holds this position because it was through Him that all things were created.

Furthermore, not only was the universe created *through and by* Him, but the universe was made *for* Him. Thus, Christ stands at the beginning of the universe and at the end of creation. He is the source of all things and the goal toward which all creation moves.

Christ is not only the source and the goal of all things, but He is also the one sustaining all things. The expression "In Him all things hold together" points to the reality that the universe owes its continuing cohesion to the sustaining work of Christ. His continual presence in the universe is not a passive coexistence. Instead, Christ is present to hold the universe together. This provides us with confidence in the present and future. Our existence is not determined by the impersonal laws of nature governed by some law of chance, as expressed in evolution theory. Our universe is held together by a personal God whose sustaining presence is realized in every nook and cranny of the universe. If the hope of our existence is based upon the actions of humanity, we are hopeless. The COVID-19 virus revealed how utterly helpless we are to sustain our existence even in the face of a microscopic problem.

Not only is our universe and the existence of our planet determined by a universally present Christ, but so are our personal lives as well. Because He is present, He knows the specific issues in our lives, and His guidance and sustaining work are individually tailored to our own lives. Christ works in our lives differently because each of us is unique, not only in our personality but also in our circumstances.

In the end, God's omnipresence is our source of confidence. Considering our assurance that Christ is the one who sustains the universe as well as each of us through His universal presence, there is no ultimate terror or fear. We do not need to fear that the world will be destroyed because we have a Redeemer who loves us enough to die for us, sustaining and directing all things through His presence.

Day 3
The God Who Is Present: Protecting His People

Read Psalm 23

I fear no evil, for You are with me. Psalm 23:4

Psalm 23 is arguably one of the most popular sections in the Bible. The imagery of green hillsides populated with grazing white sheep provides a sense of tranquility and peace. This is further enhanced by the picture of God as a shepherd, providing care for His people and the assurance of an eternal dwelling place in the house of God. This message brings comfort and encouragement to us in the midst of the most challenging times we face.

While the psalm is usually thought of in terms of God's guidance and care, in verses 4–5, we are drawn into the omniscience of God and its significance for us. In verse 4, the scene shifts from the picturesque hillsides to a dark valley, and so the mood changes from one of quiet rest to one of fearful travels. The term for the "valley of the shadow of death" comes from one word, which combines two Hebrew words: *valley* (or *shade*) and *death*. The term for shade, when used alone, is often used in a positive sense as a place for protection from the heat of the sun. However, combined with the Hebrew word for death or grave, it takes on a far more sinister meaning. Instead of a place of protection, it speaks of a far more menacing and terrifying journey. The picture is no longer of a peaceful, grass-laden hillside, but of a dark, dangerous path going through a place of extreme danger, one where evil is threatening one's very life and existence.

In such a situation, what calms the heart is the shepherd's abiding presence. David remains confident and at peace because God Himself is with him, walking beside him and providing His protective care to prevent any harm. This brings clarity to the nature of God's presence with His people, for His company offers the promise of protection and provision. The rod and staff, instruments the shepherd used both for guiding the sheep and protecting him from threatening animals, are here the source of his comfort, for the sheep knows the shepherd will protect him. So assuring is the presence of the shepherd that the psalmist even finds a place of repose and feasting in the most unlikely place—the place where his enemies are encamped around him. No matter how difficult the experiences of our lives, when we have our eyes upon God and our focus on His presence, we can have confidence and freedom from anxiety. When we take our eyes off God and start to look upon the trials that assault us, fear begins to grip us.

This week, as we delve into the riches of God's omnipresence, we find the source of great comfort. Finally, we can have peace as we walk through these uncharted waters that the uncertainty of our day has brought upon us. We do not need to fear any threat to our well-being. We do not need to become apprehensive about what the future will bring. We have a God who is present, a God who is walking beside us each step of the way, and in the end, that is all we need to know.

Day 4
The God Who Is Present: The Coming of Christ

Read Isaiah 7:10–16

She will call His name Immanuel. Isaiah 7:14

Ahaz had just heard terrifying news. The King of Aram had joined forces with the King of Israel to wage war against Judah. This was no idle threat; in verse 2, we find that "His heart and the hearts of his people shook as the trees of the forest shake with the wind." In response, God sent Isaiah to calm their fears and give them courage by assuring them that these invaders would not prevail. However, he concludes the message with a warning, "If you will not believe, you surely shall not last" (v. 9). If Ahaz and the people of Judah doubt God's promise and assurance, then they would face destruction, not because the armies were weak but because of their lack of faith. Tragically, this warning would be ignored by Ahaz, who refused to trust in God. Instead, he followed the debased worship of Baal, even having "his son pass through the fire," a euphemism for human sacrifice (2 Kings 16:3).

As a result of Ahaz's lack of faith, God again speaks to him and challenges him to ask for a sign that God would be faithful to His promise. However, Ahaz refused. Nevertheless, God gave a sign anyway. A virgin would bear a son who would be a king in the line of David and would bring God's blessing to the nation (Isaiah 7:14; 8:8,10). The name of this individual touches upon the presence of God with his people. This future king would be named "Immanuel," which means "God who is with us." This promise was then fulfilled in the coming of Christ (Matthew 1:23).

In Christ, we find the fullest expression of the presence of God. When Christ came to earth to be God's visible appearance in the flesh, He did more than just bring the reality of God's nearness to us in physical form. He became present to identify with us so that we might have a high priest who fully "sympathizes with our weaknesses" and "receive mercy and find grace to help in time of need" (Hebrews 4:15–16). In Christ, we find that God's omnipresence is not just theoretical and abstract but relational and personal. He is present to establish a personal relationship with us and bring deliverance and salvation from a plight worse than death.

As we go through times of difficulty, we have the assurance that Christ is not only present with us, but that He understands what we are facing and desires to provide us help and assistance in our greatest needs. To live with the awareness of the omnipresence of God is to live with the understanding that He desires to be in a relationship with us—a relationship grounded in openness and trust. Therefore, as you go throughout today's activities, be aware of His presence and be in continual conversation with Him, seeking His guidance and direction. Christ is not merely present with you to observe your life. He is Emmanuel, "God with us," every step of the way, guiding, protecting, and relating to you as a friend.

Day 5
The Presence of Christ: Being Present in the World

Read Matthew 28:16–20; Acts 1:6–8

I am with you always. Matthew 28:20

While God is present in every corner of the universe, He remains invisible to the human eye. For a period, God did enter our world in time and space through the person of Christ. While that was crucial to our understanding of God, we still live in a world where God remains invisible. But God has not left the world with no visible presence, for the church becomes His visual representation to people.

In Matthew 28 and Acts 1, God appoints the church to be His universal presence in the world. As Christ comes to the end of His physical ministry within the world, He calls the church to become present throughout the nations. However, just as His presence has a relational focus, the church is to have a relational presence in which we are to convey His truth to all people. We are to go throughout the world, calling people into a relationship with God. Yet, we do not do this alone, for we have the promise of Christ's presence with us. When He states that He is always with us to the end of the age, we have the assurance of His nearness and involvement in our lives and ministries.

The crisis we face on a personal level is never in isolation from others. When we live in the presence of Christ, we then have the opportunity to be the presence of God to others. To do this, we need to be intentional in our relationships with people. In our struggles, we have the opportunity to reveal Christ to the people around us. While we have certainty in an uncertain world, people around us struggle to discover a sense of normality and security. That comes when we share the gospel with others. Peter challenges us to "[a]lways [be] ready to make a defense to everyone who asks you to give an account for the hope that is in you" (1 Peter 3:15).

The question then is how we can demonstrate the presence of Christ to the world. First, we can connect with people. There are several ways to communicate with people. Have dinner together. Share a mutual interest in a hobby. Take to time to give people a phone call. Talk with your neighbors across the fence. Second, invite people to join you at a church service. Have a neighbor-hood party. Share links to Sunday services with your neighbors. Third, pray for people and ask how you can pray for them. People are troubled, and prayer is an opportunity to demonstrate that we care about them. Last, be aware of people's physical and emo-tional needs.

We need to be sensitive to these people and minister to their needs. When others are going through trials, spend time asking God to give you opportunities to be the presence of God to those around you. Then, look for those opportunities and be ready to share the reality of God's presence with them.

The Unchanging God

Jesus Christ is the same yesterday and today and forever.

Hebrews 13:8

We live in a world of constant change. From the weather to the circumstances we face, life continues to change, sometimes with astonishing rapidity that we struggle to keep up. Because our world is continuously shifting and continually fluctuating, it is hard to understand that God never changes. He is the one constant in a transitory universe. In James 1:17, James describes God as the "Father of Lights, with whom there is no variation or shifting shadow." There is no variation with God, a term that speaks of a change in the nature or character of an event or person. The phrase is even stronger in the original than in English; literally, it reads, "in association with God there is not one variation." This is further highlighted in the following statement, "or shifting shadow." The idea is that there is no changing or reversing the direction of the course God has chosen. Therefore, when we speak of the immutability of God, we are referring to the truth that God is unchanging in His being, nature, purposes, and promises.

Often today, we want to humanize God. Because we are continually changing, we believe that God also changes. Consequently, some want to see the Old Testament's God as different from the God of the New Testament. For example, God is angry and judging in the Old Testament, but God becomes loving and gracious in the New Testament. However, to say that God can change is to imply that He is imperfect and flawed and thus needs to change to become increasingly perfect. Or, if He is perfect, then He would change to become imperfect. Therefore, changing His character or His purpose and plans would imply some level of imperfection with God.

To speak of the immutability of God, we must affirm two central truths. First, God does not change in His person or character, for He is perfect. This the psalmist proclaims (and later the writer of Hebrews affirms in relationship to Christ's being): "But You are the same, and Your years will not come to an end" (Psalm 102:27). In contrast to the universe, which is changing and decaying as time marches forward (v. 28), God remains constant. His character and being are unaltered by time and circumstances. "For I, the LORD, do not change" (Malachi 3:6). As A. W. Pink affirmed, "He cannot change for the better for He is already perfect and being perfect He cannot change to the worse."[6]

Second, God does not change in His purposes and plans. "The counsel of the LORD stands forever, the plans of His heart from generation to generation" (Psalm 33:11). If God changed His plans, it would imply one of two things: 1) that God did not know the future and thus, because of changes He did not anticipate, He had to change His plans, or 2) God made a mistake in His goals and so needs to alter them. In both cases, God becomes imperfect and less than God.

His unchanging nature is what distinguishes God from all creation. While we are becoming, God *is*. This is the foundation of our hope and the grounds for our faith. That God is unchanging stands in stark contrast to the instability of man. It is the

---

6. Arthur.W. Pink, *The Immutability of God*, http://www.reformedreader.org/aog04.htm, accessed 9/6/2021.

immutability of God that gives us confidence in the face of trials, for our hope is grounded in the unchanging promises of God (James 1:12). How often do we make promises that we cannot keep because we are always in a state of change? Sometimes we forget the promises. Sometimes we make a promise, but the circumstances change so that we cannot fulfill that promise. Occasionally, we cannot complete our pledge because we do not have the ability we thought we possessed at the time. Sometimes, we fail to fulfill a promise because we are broken people marred by sin, and we fail to keep our word; not so with God. God does not change, and because He does not change, His Word is always faithful, and His promises are always sure. Therefore, we can trust in His unchanging plan. With God, there is never a need for "Plan B." There is never a need to change or alter the course of action. This is why we can also have confidence that the God who cared for His people in the Bible will care for us even today.

Day 1
The Unchanging God: Our Hope in Changing Times

Read Psalm 102

But you are the same, and your years will not come to an end. Psalm 102:27

Psalm 102 is a psalm of lament. The lament psalms were written in the context of trials and adversity (see also Psalm 13, 22, 51). These psalms were written when people were confronted with a crisis that interrupted their daily life and brought significant discomfort and spiritual confusion. When we read the psalms of lament, they shock us with their blunt honesty before God. Expressing deep emotion, pain, and anger, they convey their confusion of why God was not acting on the psalmists' behalf. However, the author of Psalm 102 does not leave us in the throes of despair, for intrinsic to the lament is a confession of trust and a vow to praise God for His deliverance.

Psalm 102 contains all the elements we find in a psalm of lament. First, in verses 2–11 and 13–17 we see a crisis confronting the psalmist. Second, we see the honest complaint before God (vv. 9–11, 23). Third, due to God's abandonment of him, his enemies have attacked and taunted him mercilessly (v. 8). Finally, just when we might expect the psalmist to abandon his faith in God, he instead reaffirms his trust (vv. 12–22, 25–28) and so brings his prayer before God (vv. 1–2, 24).

What moves the psalmist away from his pain and complaint and into confident trust in God? The answer lies in verse 27 (see also verse 12). He finds his confidence in the unchanging nature of God, which stands in stark contrast to the decay and change we see in the world around us. In the Hebrew text, the words are more striking. The first line reads, "And You are He." The words echo the thought given in Psalm 100:3: "Know that the LORD Himself is God." The idea is that He is the same God, the one who is—the one who does not change. He is not the God who was, nor the God who will be, but the God who *is*.

God stands in contrast to the physical world, which suffers from decay, change, and decline. God is the constant one. His essence and being are never altered, either by himself or by some external cause. This is the anchor point in a world driven by the winds of circumstances. No matter how much life around us changes and circumstances beyond our control seem to blow us aimlessly around, God remains the constant one. For the psalmist, this was his comfort; the God who delivered His people in the past is the same God who would bring deliverance to him. Because God does not change, we can rest in the same assurance today. The God who acted in the Old Testament on behalf of His people is the same God who acts today on our behalf. Therefore, just as the psalmist made his prayer to God with blunt honesty and confident faith, so we can also come before Him in prayer. As you go throughout this week and feel the pressures of the struggles you are facing, be open and honest with God regarding your circumstances, tribulations, and doubts, and then pray with confidence that He will always hear and respond in His perfect timing.

Day 2
The Unchanging God: The God Who Always Forgives

Read Malachi 3:1–7

For I, the LORD, do not change. Malachi 3:6

Malachi was the last of the Old Testament prophets. He was sent to the people of Israel to bring one final warning for them to turn from their sin. In 722 BC, the northern nation of Israel had been cast into exile because of their idolatry. In 586 BC, the southern nation of Judah would follow them into captivity. Time and time again, God had sent prophets to warn them of their impending judgment if they did not repent. Yet, they callously refused to listen, and so they were cast into exile. However, God did not abandon them, and in 516 BC, and again in 458 BC and 444 BC, God would move in the hearts of their captors to allow the people of Israel to return to the land promised to them by God.

Even after their punishment and restoration, they continued to disobey God. So, once again, God would send prophets to warn them of their sin, but like before, they continued to ignore God's appeal. Malachi was the last prophet sent, bringing both a word of warning and a word of hope. In chapters 1 and 2, Malachi rebukes the unfaithfulness of the priests and the people. Then, in chapter 3:1–5, he warns them that God will again come in discipline and judgment as He seeks to purge Israel of their immorality and idolatry.

Amid this warning, Malachi offers a glimmer of hope that even though Israel would experience the devastation of God's discipline, He will not destroy them. However, it is why God would not consume them that captures our attention and gives us hope today. Their hope, and our hope today, are grounded in the unchanging nature of God. When God pledged His commitment and promise to Abraham, Moses, and David that He would establish the nation of Israel and that they would be the source of His blessing to the world, He bound himself to it. Regardless of their unfaithfulness, He would still pour out His goodness upon them when they returned in repentance. God does not change, and neither do His promises. Therefore, even despite their sin, God would remain faithful to the promise that He would not destroy them in judgment.

He is the same God who has pledged His faithfulness to us and His commitment to accept us back into fellowship no matter how great our sin (see 1 John 1:9). Even when we have walked away from Him in rebellion and indifference, He is always ready and willing to accept us back and pour out His blessings upon us. No matter how far we may stray from His Word, He is still there and available and ready to restore our lives. In times of adversity and difficulties, we should pause and reevaluate our relationship with God. It is a time for spiritual reflection to ensure that we are walking in obedience to God and in fellowship with Him. Because He never changes, today, you have the promise that He is always ready to restore and forgive even your greatest sin. Today, ask God to give you a desire to know Him, and He promises that He will fulfill that prayer.

Day 3
The Unchanging God: He Does Not Change His Promises

Read Numbers 23:18–26

God is not a man that He should lie, nor a son of man, that He should repent. Numbers 23:19

Balak was frustrated. He had recruited Balaam, a for-hire pagan prophet, to pronounce a curse upon Israel in hopes of weakening their threat against Moab. But in the first attempt, God superimposed His will, and instead of pronouncing a curse, Balaam pronounced a blessing. Not one to give up easily, Balak thought that perhaps the problem stemmed from the location rather than the message. Because they believed that the gods were geographically confined to specific areas, Balak reasoned that a venue change would enable Balaam to pronounce a curse. However, once again, Balak and Balaam were thwarted in their plan. In Numbers 23:19, we find the reason why Balaam could not pronounce a curse: Because God is unchanging. Once He has made a promise, He will be faithful to fulfill that promise. Even a false prophet, who presumes to speak for God, cannot change the promises God has made to Israel to bring them into the promised land. Unlike man who must repent (i.e. to change one's mind about a course of action or truth), God does not repent, for God never makes a mistake or error.

The unchanging promises of God are a comfort for us in times of uncertainty. God has given us promises of peace and assurance in the face of all the struggles we face. While He does not promise to keep our life free from trials, He does promise that He has an eternal purpose in these struggles. God promises that He will not abandon us in times of adversity (2 Corinthians 4:8–9). He will give us the strength to deal with every circumstance, whether in times of prosperity or difficulties (Philippians 4:12–13). We have the promise that we have eternal life and that after suffering, He will make us strong, firm, and steadfast (1 Peter 5:10). We know that God is using every situation to strengthen our faith (James 1:2–4). He promises to listen to our prayers and respond to us by giving us mercy and grace during our troubles (Hebrews 4:14–16). And the list could go on. It is estimated that there are between three to seven thousand promises in the Bible.

These promises, made over two thousand years ago, are still just as relevant and valid as they were when first given by Christ and His prophets. We can hold to these promises in both our present and future because God does not change. Time and circumstances do not affect either His being or His purpose. Therefore, we find the same strength and hope in these promises as did previous generations of believers. When you start feeling the pressure of the uneasiness of our present circumstances, spend time reading the Bible and identifying and affirming the promises that God has given you. Then ask God to provide you with the strength to find your confidence and security in them rather than the circumstances surrounding you.

Day 4
The Unchanging God: The God Who Carries Us

Read Isaiah 46:3–7

You who have been borne by Me from birth and have been carried from the womb, even to your old age I will be the same, and even to your graying years, I will bear you. Isaiah 46:3

Israel was continually lured by the false gods of the people surrounding them. Part of our sin nature is that we desire to recreate gods that conform to our perspective. We want a God who agrees with our thoughts and values. Such was the case of Israel. But in Isaiah 46:5–7, we find the folly of pursuing gods of our own creation. When we conform God to our thinking, God becomes a powerless being. While we do not create a physical idol, like those in Isaiah's day, in the end, we are no different. Today we see people belittle prayer and instead place their trust in the god of human wisdom and ingenuity. We reject the moral standards of the God of the Bible to pursue the gods of sexuality and personal pleasure. We even sacrifice our children on the altar of personal choice and convenience. However, any god who conforms to our views is too small and powerless in the face of the onslaught of the issues we face in life. Just like the golden idols of Babylon, we may cry to them, but they cannot answer and cannot deliver us from our distress (v. 7).

In contrast to the gods of our making is the God of Israel. He is the God who carries us from the womb until our old age, and He remains the same, unchanging in His purpose and care for us (v. 4). God remains the same, unequaled in His being and might. The word *bear* has the idea of enduring something difficult, whether on one's own behalf or on behalf of someone else. In other words, God undertakes on our behalf, and He takes our burdens and places them upon Himself. Throughout our lives, no matter what we are facing, God upholds and sustains us.

Furthermore, He will deliver us—that is, He saves us from any ruin, destruction, or harm that may befall us. By repeating this promise, God provides further assurance that He will faithfully fulfill this pledge. Thus, we have the guarantee that God's care for us will never end and that His care is always available. His care stands in stark contrast to the idols we create that cannot even rescue themselves, much less us.

Throughout the history of God's people, we find continual examples of when God provided His deliverance and care for His people. He sustained Abraham when he left his family in Ur to travel to the unknown region of God's choosing. God carried Joseph through rejection by his family, slavery, and imprisonment. He delivered David when Saul was seeking his life. He provided spiritual protection for the disciples while they were confused during Christ's arrest and crucifixion. When we see the great acts of God caring for His people, it is easy for us to think that these events only occurred in biblical times and that God does not act the same today. Yet, in verse 4, Isaiah gives us the assurance that God doesn't change, and the same God who worked on behalf of His people in the Bible is the same God who acts on your behalf today. No matter what happens in the world today, you have the assurance that the unchanging God is still upholding you with His unseen hand. When you start becoming fearful, rest in His unalterable promise and character.

Day 5
The Unchanging God: The God Who Fulfills His Purpose

Read Isaiah 46:8-13

Truly, I have spoken; truly I will bring it to pass.
Isaiah 46:8-13

God is unchanging in His purpose. He calls Israel to remember the past and to be reminded that He is a God unparalleled in His power. Unlike the idols who cannot even care for themselves and are indifferent to the people worshiping them, God not only has a purpose for His people, but He has the power and ability to achieve that purpose. He will still accomplish His plan for them (vv. 10–11). Therefore, even though they have rebelled and distanced themselves from God, He is always near them and is willing to bring salvation to them (vv. 12–13).

God's involvement in our lives is more than just as a cheerleader who shouts words of encouragement. From eternity past, He established a purpose for the universe and our individual lives. That purpose is realized in our salvation and in His desire to impart His righteousness and image in us. Because He established His intention, we can have confidence in the present. Nothing is happening in the present that threatens or alters God's redemptive plan for our lives. Instead, He orchestrates events so that the effects our circumstances have upon us are part of His grand design to move us in the direction of His redemptive goal.

Consequently, we are just as secure today in God's plan as we were before these events unfolded. If God changed, if circumstances altered His purpose, then we would have reason to fear, for we would have no assurance that His plan for us will be accomplished. However, in His unchanging nature, we have peace and absolute confidence that no matter what happens to us, He will achieve His eternal goal of transforming us to be like Christ—and for us to carry His message to a lost world. Consequently, we no longer need to be apprehensive about today's events.

When you become anxious about the events outside your control, remember that God controls all circumstances and that He has a plan for your life that is certain and unchanging. God's greatest desire is that you would "know Christ and be found in Him, not having a righteousness of your own, but that which is through faith in Christ, that you might know Him and the power of His resurrection" (Philippians 3:8–11). Nothing can change or thwart that plan for those who walk in obedience to Him.

The Love of God

I will heal their apostasy, I will love them freely . . .
I will be like the dew to Israel; He will blossom like
the lily.

Hosea 14:4–5

O ne of the most fundamental of all human needs is the
need for love. We can face many trials and difficult
circumstances, but we will quickly wither and plunge
into despair when we feel unloved by others. Yet, for all our
need for love, we often struggle to understand what love is. We
view love as conditional, based upon the response of the recipi-
ent. Love becomes an emotion that changes over time. We often
render love superficial and trite. We say we love our spouses in
the same breath that we affirm our love for our pets.

To understand the love of God, we must think differently. We
must understand the nature of love, not from our culture, but
from the instruction of Scripture, which points to the nature of
love as well as the meaning and significance of God's love. The
word that Scripture uses to describe love is the Greek word *agape*.
In contrast to our emotionally driven love, this love originates in
the will, involving a deliberate decision to place value and worth
upon the other and place their well-being above our own. Driven
by one's willful commitment, biblical love is unconditional. It is

not based on the worthiness of the object but solely upon the grace of the giver. Thus, we find that we are to love our enemies.

Furthermore, biblical love is sacrificial. It involves the willingness to place others' needs above our own and sacrifice one's desires and well-being to benefit the other. In contrast to the fickle nature of our current view of love, biblical love is grounded in a covenant relationship in which there is complete and unconditional loyalty and faithfulness. When we speak of God as a God of love, we affirm that God is not just the source of love, but He is the one who defines love. It is intrinsic to His nature and is interwoven within all His other attributes. While affirming the love of God, we must also accept the justice and wrath of God. While His justice demands the certainty of judgment, His love motivates God to provide a means by which His justice may be satisfied and His judgement averted. When we speak of God's love, we affirm that He is a God of love and eternally gives of himself to others. He freely acts on our behalf to pour out His blessing upon us and give us what is good. This should cause us to pause in wonderment that the God of the universe, the triune God as seen in the Father, the Son, and the Spirit, give of Themselves to bring us genuine joy and happiness, and They will continue to do so for all eternity.

This love has three important implications for us today. First, it motivates the redemptive work of Christ. Often, we neglect to understand the cost of God's love for us. Our salvation cost the Father the one thing that was dearest to Him (His Son) so that we might obtain what is most valuable for us (our salvation). He gave up everything to obtain nothing so that we, who have nothing, might gain everything. He then gave us His Spirit to be with us and guide us so that we might not only be saved from sin but also live in fellowship with Him.

Second, His love removes our fear and provides security for us. Because of His love for us, there is never a reason to fear. We no longer need to be afraid of God or that we will lose our standing before God. If God loved us in our worst possible state, then we have had the assurance that He will never reject us in the future. This is the irony of our understanding of His love. Those who reject His offer of salvation and are objects of His judgment minimize His justice, so they have no fear of God.

On the other hand, we, who are the object of His love, tend to minimize His love and still live in fear rather than joy. Rather than resting in His love, we still feel that we must somehow earn His favor. To fully understand God's love is to be free from the fear of judgment.

Last, because He loves us unconditionally and ultimately, we are free to love others unconditionally and freely. Central in our expression of love and commitment to God is our love for others. We can give to others, even amid our struggles, because we know that God will take care of us. It becomes the expression of our loyalty to Him.

While we do not understand why He allows adversity in our love, we can trust God to be motivated by His love for us and that everything He does has our best interests in mind. We may not understand or see the end, but we can trust in the loving God who does.

Day 1
The Love of God: He Loves Us at Our Worst

Read Romans 5:6–11

God demonstrates His own love toward us, in that while we were yet sinners, Christ died for us. Romans 5:8

It is easy to love others when they are at their best and they treat us kindly. However, when they are at their worst and most unloving, then love is truly tested. Loving others is always measured, not by how we love and care for those who are friends but by how we respond and treat our enemies. How do we love others who have treated us heartlessly and deeply hurt us? This is when love is ultimately tested.

To understand the depth of God's love for us, we need to realize that He loved us when we were the most unlovable. In Romans 5, Paul is setting forth the results of our justification. The word "justify" is a legal term whereby we are declared righteous and innocent in the sight of the law. Instead of being pronounced guilty as lawbreakers, we are now declared righteous. This new status is not achieved by our merits, for we stand guilty as sinners. Instead, this status is achieved through the death of Christ, who paid the penalty for our sin and satisfied the justice of God (v. 6).

In verse 8, we find the expression of the full depth of God's love for us. The motive behind the work of Christ is the immeasurable love of God. This love He demonstrates not when we are making our appeal to Him and pleading for forgiveness but while we are still hostile toward Him. He loves us when we are the sworn enemies of God (v. 10).

However, Paul argues from the greater to the lesser to give us hope and confidence in God's continual love and care for us. If God demonstrates His love for us when we are His enemies, then how much more will He continue to love us when we are now reconciled back to Him? The word *reconciliation* means to be restored to a friendly relationship with someone after a presumed wrong, which in this case is not a wrong that God has done to us, but a wrong we had done when we rejected God's word and rebelled against Him. Because of reconciliation, instead of being His enemies, we are now considered His friends. The reason for this change in status is not anything we have done; it is because of what He did for us through the death of Christ (v. 10).

In times of struggle, it is easy to become discouraged and begin to question God's love for us. It is easy to feel abandoned by God. Yet, in this darkness of gloom, we find this light of hope—that God loves us completely, immeasurably, unconditionally, and eternally. In the next few moments, spend time giving thanks to God for His love for you and then reflect on the significance of His love, especially in these days of uncertainty.

Day 2
The Love of God: His Love Is Faithful

Read Isaiah 54:4–10

For the mountains may be removed, and the hills may shake, but My lovingkindness will not be removed from you. Isaiah 54:10

The word lovingkindness comes from the Hebrew word *hesed*. The word itself was rich in Hebrew thought and their understanding of God. The Hebrew word speaks of an unfailing kind of love, and thus it was used concerning God's love, which is grounded in His faithfulness to the promises He made with His people. When God made a covenant to align Himself relationally with His people—to be their God—He bound Himself to an eternal relationship with them and the obligations He made. Thus, we find in verse 10 that because of His love for His people, He would never break the covenant He made with them even though the world itself might be chaotic. His love is surer and more steadfast than the ground we walk. In Isaiah 54, Isaiah gives a message of hope even as Israel experiences the discipline of God. He warns them that there will be a time when His outburst of anger is felt, but in the end, His lovingkindness will move Him to have compassion for them (v. 8). So great is His promise that even though a mighty earthquake should shake the whole earth, His lovingkindness will remain, and they will continue to be the object of His steadfast love.

This kind of love contrasts the transitory nature of commitment and love that we see today. Today, marriage is no longer grounded in a commitment "until death do us part," but has become "until life do us part." When life becomes complicated and our commitment to one another is tested, we find it easier to abandon the marriage than do the hard work of changing our attitudes and actions. We demonstrate little of the faithfulness of love in other relationships as well. When someone hurts us and betrays our loyalty, we would rather cut off the ties than forgive unconditionally and remain committed to maintaining the relationship. Commitment and faithfulness in relationships are never easy. This is what makes it so hard for us to understand God's *hesed*—that He will remain faithful and committed to our relationship with Him no matter how much we may offend Him and betray our commitment to Him.

No matter what happens in life, no matter how much we are "afflicted, storm-tossed and without comfort" (v. 11), we have the assurance that God's compassion and love for us will not be removed. Because of His faithful love, we have the guarantee that when God makes us a promise, He will fulfill it. The idea that all the mountains and the whole of creation would be "removed" seems unimaginable, but far more unthinkable is the notion that God's steadfast love would be "removed" (the same Hebrew word is used in both instances) from His people. This is our comfort and source of confidence, that no matter how shaken our world is, God's love for us is never shaken. God is always faithful to us, even when we, like Israel during Isaiah's day, are not loyal to Him. This is what should drive us continually back to Him. In our times of sin, guilt, or apprehension concerning life's uncertainties, we can flee to Him because He remains committed to His promises in His Word to love us continually and unconditionally.

Day 3
The Love of God: The God Who Delights in Us

Read Zephaniah 3:12–20

He will exult over you with joy, He will be quiet in His love, He will rejoice over you with shouts of joy. Zephaniah 3:17

When we love someone, we find joy in being with them and rejoice in their accomplishments and happiness. We enjoy taking a hike together with our spouse. Part of life's enjoyment is sharing life with someone and weeping when they weep and rejoicing when they rejoice. So also, as a parent, we find great joy when seeing the accomplishments of our children. We rejoice with them when they cross the podium to get their diploma. We share their happiness when they stand before a pastor and exchange their vows with the person they love. We share their joy when they weep at the wonder of the birth of their first child.

Sometimes it is difficult for us to grasp the depth of God's love for us. Because we associate love with touch and face-to-face interaction, God seems remote and distant because we cannot touch, see, or feel Him like we do with people. As a result, the concept of His unfailing love for us seems abstract and academic

rather than personal and involved. Yet, amazingly when we examine Scripture, we not only see God's love for us expressed in
His giving of Himself to make us happy, but we also discover
that He finds joy in us. Zephaniah concludes his prophetic message with the promise of Israel's restoration. Considering Israel's
redemption, he calls upon Israel to shout for joy, for God will
no longer discipline Israel but will give them victory over their
enemies. No longer will they be fearful, for God is now in their
midst.

To capture the delight that God has for His people, Zephaniah,
in verse 17, uses three definitive statements. First, "He will exult
over you with joy." This phrase expresses the delight that God
receives when He blesses His people. Just as a husband finds joy
in his wife and parents find joy in the life and accomplishments
of their children, so God rejoices over us.

The following thought is even more surprising. The phrase
"He will be quiet in His love" speaks of the quiet contemplation
of love that one has for another. The picture is of a lover who
is sitting quietly, just enjoying thinking of his love. Usually, the
image is of people silently meditating upon God, but here God
is quietly meditating on us! That the God of the universe sits in
quiet reflection of His love for us is beyond our comprehension.

The final phrase provides an even more astonishing picture of
God bursting into song to express His love for His people. The
phrase "shouts of joy" refers to the act of singing vocal music.
Sometimes, when we meditate upon God's goodness and love for
us, we will break out into a song, singing a favorite chorus or
hymn as an expression of our wonder of God's love. However,
this is not people bursting forth in songs of worship and praise
for God; it is God Himself bursting forth in a love song for us!

One writer summarizes the verse this way: "To consider
Almighty God sinking in contemplations of love over a once
wretched human being can hardly be absorbed by the human

mind."[7] Yet this is the picture presented—that God finds joy in His love for us. Such love is incomprehensible. When circumstances press in around us, and we feel discouraged and abandoned by people and even by God, remember that God sings for joy because of His love for you.

Day 4
The Love of God: His Inseparable Love

Read Romans 8:31–39

Who will separate us from the love of Christ?
Romans 8:35

Romans 8 provides great insight into God's redemptive work even amid the struggles we face in life. In verse 18, Paul concludes that the suffering of the present pales in comparison to the unfathomable glory awaiting us in heaven. While all of creation presently suffers under the destructive effects of a broken world, it is only temporary, for there will come a time when all things will be fully renewed. This gives us confidence in the face of the trials we encounter in the present, for we know that He is orchestrating His plan in such a way that everything accomplishes an eternal purpose. Since God is on our side, there is nothing that can destroy us.

As we read through this passage, we find two indisputable facts upon which Paul rests his faith. First, his confidence is grounded in the person of Christ who died for us to free us from

---

7. Kenneth L. Barker, *The New Testament Commentary*, vol. 20 (Nashville: Broadman and Holman Publishers, 1999), 497.

any condemnation. This work of Christ provides for us the proof of God's care and concern for us.

The second reason for Paul's confidence, and the one that we want to focus on, is the abiding love of Christ. Through Christ, we have the assurance that nothing can separate us from the love of God. The word *separate* (v. 35) has the idea of something that would isolate or cause estrangement from another. In contrast to our personal relationships, which can be threatened and destroyed by our actions, others' actions, or even circumstances beyond our control, nothing causes any distance between ourselves and the loving Father. In verse 35, Paul looks at all the suffering we encounter in life, from distress to the attacks of others, and yet he remains confident that it is not a threat to God's love for us. In verses 38–39, Paul expands this search to the whole universe. He gives a litany of superpowers we might encounter in the universe, yet none of them are a threat to the attentive love of Christ. Apart from God Himself, angels are the most powerful beings, yet they are powerless to come between God and us. Likewise, with its inescapable certainty, death is incapable of causing even a fleeting separation in our relationship with God. Even time, which continues to march relentlessly forward, bringing constant change, is insufficient to change God's love. Not even hell itself can alter His love. While each of these may destroy and separate us from our family and friends and those dear to us, they remain impotent to loosen the grip of His love for us.

As we struggle with circumstances, we have the assurance that one remains continuously by our side, one who is closer than a brother, who loves and cares for us immeasurably more than we can imagine, and that is God Himself. While we may long for human companionship and fellowship with others, we still have the confidence that God loves us completely and continually. At every moment, you are enveloped in it, sustained by it, upheld and encouraged through it, and hopeful because of it, for there is nothing that can cause even the slightest momentary separation in your relationship with God. God's love is inseparable.

Day 5
The Love of God: Loving Him in Return

Read John 14:18–24; Deuteronomy 6:4–9

If anyone loves Me, he will keep My word. John 14:23

If God's love for us is expressed in His giving of Himself for our good and ultimate happiness, how do we express our love for God? This is no idle question, but goes to the very heart of what it means to be a disciple of Christ and what it means to be genuinely spiritual. Christ calls us to be in a relationship with Him, but what impact does this relationship have upon our lives? Today, we equate spirituality with emotionalism. We go to church, desiring to be moved emotionally by the music. We want sermons that entertain us, make us feel good, and affirm us but make no demands upon us. Paul warns Timothy of the dangers of the church developing a feel-good, me-centered theology that makes us comfortable rather than transformed when he writes, "For the time will come when they will not endure sound doctrine: but wanting to have their ears tickled, they will accumulate for themselves teachers in accordance to their own desires" (2 Timothy 4:3). We want a religion that affirms our lifestyle rather than transforms our total being.

In contrast to this, the words of Christ call us to a different perspective of what it means to love Him genuinely. The measure of our love for God is seen in our conformity to His Word.

Six times in John 14 and 15, Christ emphasizes that genuine love for Him is revealed in our obedience (14:15, 21, 23–24; 15:5, 14). However, this is not a new revolutionary teaching of Jesus. Instead, it is an outgrowth of the Old Testament itself. In Deuteronomy 6:4–9, God calls Israel's people to love Him with all their heart, soul, and might. The meaning is given in the following statement, "These words which I am commanding you today shall be on your heart" (v. 6). To love God with all our heart is to integrate His commandments into all aspects of life (vv. 7–9). We are to teach and model obedience to the Scriptures to our children through our words and actions in every facet of life. When God commands them to bind His commands on their hands and as frontals on their foreheads, He emphasizes that His law governs every action and thought. It is the governing principle in their home and when they go out into society to conduct their business. Anything less than this reveals a heart of rebellion rather than love.

The greatest act of love a child can express is obeying his parents and striving to be like them. The same is true in our relationship with God. To truly love God, we must be devoted to His word, striving to become like Him. We must allow His Word to shape our lives and govern our world. When we go through trials, they serve to strip away everything superficial and force us to examine our lives to determine what is truly important. When we get down to brass tacks, we find the only thing that matters is walking in obedience to Christ and becoming like Him. In times of adversity, the most critical question to ask is *who*: Whom am I becoming? Whom am I following and obeying? Whom am I influencing? Am I following Christ and obeying Him, or am I following others, the world, or even my selfish desires? At the end of life, your relationship and obedience to Christ are the only things that are genuinely important.

The Goodness of God

*Deep calls to deep at the sound of Your waterfalls,
All Your breakers, and Your waves have rolled over
me. The Lord will command His lovingkindness in
the daytime, and His song will be with me in the
night.*

Psalm 42:7–8

When we mine into the riches of God's character, the one diamond we discover that radiates with beauty to our eyes is the goodness of God. As we gaze upon its beauty, we find that it stands at the heart of all His activities and actions. However, like any dazzling diamond, this stone is multifaced in its beauty, and it captures our attention as we gaze upon it. For in the goodness of God, we find three words that are used together to capture its essence. Like the brilliance of a precious stone, these three words have different nuances. Still, together they serve to give us a complete picture of the goodness and kindness of God that He demonstrates toward us.

The first word that provides a glimpse into this goodness is the word *mercy*. At the heart of mercy is the idea that God shows His kindness and concern for us when we are in severe need and severe distress. This causes us to look inward. For us to truly understand His mercy, we need to understand the depth of our misery. When sin entered the world, it brought devastating consequences for all humanity. We see this every day as we look about us and see the events of our own lives. God created us with the intention that we would be in a perfect setting where we would enjoy His daily presence and blessings. However, in our folly, we rebelled and sought freedom from God. Instead of enjoying His blessing, we became slaves to death and destruction. Even though God could have left us in that condition, He mercifully acted on our behalf.

His mercy then moved Him to act with grace, which is the second aspect of God's goodness. The nuance of grace captures God's undeserved love and compassion for those who forfeited it and deserved the very opposite. Because of our rebellion, we deserve His judgment, "for all have sinned and come short of the glory of God." However, God instead bestowed His grace by providing us the gift of salvation so that we might obtain what we could never merit on our own—the gift of eternal life.

The third facet of this diamond is His infinite patience. God, in His goodness, withholds the punishment of our sin for a period to allow us the opportunity to seek Him. While God is a God of mercy and grace, He is also just and holy. Because of His justice, sin demands a penalty. However, in His patience, He does not immediately rain down His judgment. Instead, He gives us every opportunity to seek Him.

His goodness is not only freely bestowed upon us, but is abundantly lavished upon us (Ephesians 1:7–8). The word *lavish* means to provide something in great abundance. In other words, He has bestowed His grace, mercy, and patience upon us to the extent that they go far beyond what was needed. Not only does He cover the depth of our sin, but He further graciously gives us every spiritual blessing. As we investigate the pages of Scripture, we see a glimpse into the extent of His gifts:

• He has given us His love (Romans 5:5)

- He has given us peace amid turmoil (John 14:27)
- He has given us joy in life (John 15:11)
- He has given us strength in times of difficulty (Philippians 4:13)
- He has given us guidance and clarity through His Word (2 Timothy 3:16)
- He has given us the presence and comfort of His Spirit (John 14)
- He has assured us of our salvation (Romans 8:38–39)
- He has given us the promise of eternal life (1 John 5:11)
- He has assured us of His divine help in times of need (Hebrews 4:16)
- He has forgiven our sin (Ephesians 1:7)
- He has given us an eternal inheritance (Ephesians 1:11–12)
- He has given us His seal of ownership (Ephesians 1:13–14)

And the list could go on (it has been estimated that there are over fifty spiritual blessings mentioned in the book of Ephesians alone). However, the greatest act of His goodness is that He has given us the position of His children. Just saving us from the clutches of hell was an act of grace beyond measure, but the depth of His goodness was demonstrated when He elevated us to a position in His family. Thus, we became co-heirs with Christ (Romans 8:11–17). This defies understanding. We, who have rebelled against Him and deserve only judgment, are now placed in a position of having the same status and rights Christ enjoys before the Father.

Considering all He has done for us, the one thing we should never question, no matter how many struggles we face, is His goodness toward us. We may not understand why He allows adversity to come upon us, but we can never doubt the grace and mercy that He has already given us.

Day 1
The Grace of God

Read Psalm 103

The LORD is compassionate and gracious . . . He has not dealt with us according to our sins nor rewarded us according to our iniquities. Psalm 103:8,10

David was one person who could identify with our struggle with guilt and failure and our regret for the past. While we often think of David as the giant-killing man of stalwart faith, in reality David was anything but. Like us, David struggled with temptation, discouragement, and failure in both his personal life and his relationship with God. The list of David's sins and failures would cause any search committee looking to find the next pastor for their church to reject his resume. He committed adultery and then murdered the woman's husband to cover up his sin. He struggled with depression and discouragement when Saul was pursuing him to take his life. At times he had waves of uncontrollable anger, which in one case almost led to murder (only the intervention of a wise woman prevented him from enacting his revenge). He lied to those offering him protection. He failed as a parent by not correctly disciplining his sons even when they committed rape and incest. Because of these failures, his family would eventually be ripped apart by jealousy and hatred. His inability to trust in God's protection resulted in a deadly plague that afflicted the people. The list goes on.

When David wrote of the wonders of God's grace in Psalm 103, he did so from the perspective of one who truly understood the guilt of sin. David was painfully aware of his spiritual and moral failures. However, the guilt did not lead him away from

God; it drove him to God, searching for forgiveness and cleansing. What distinguished David from many others was not the excellence of his conduct but his response to his failures. Instead of trying to excuse his sin, he cast himself before God to seek mercy and grace. Thus, when David wrote Psalm 103, he did so from the context of one who knew the depth of his failure and the supremacy of God's grace.

To understand the graciousness of God, we need to realize that we have rebelled against God and broken His commandments. As a result, we deserve only divine judgment. However, God demonstrated His grace when He did not give us what we deserve (judgment and punishment). Instead, He looked upon us with favor and forgiveness. Thus, in verses 10–12, David states that God does not reward us according to our iniquities, but instead removes our guilt as far as the east is from the west.

Sometimes when we go through trials and tragedies, we begin to wonder if God is punishing us. Deep down, we are fully aware of our sin and guilt before God, so we attribute our struggles to divine displeasure. However, if we have sought God's forgiveness, He has promised that He will "pardon all your iniquities, heal all your diseases; redeem your life from the pit, and crown you with lovingkindness and compassion" (vv. 3–4).

While God's grace does not insulate you from the trials and pains of life (we still live in a broken world affected by the reality of sin), you do have the promise that when these things happen, it is not because of His anger or wrath, or as punishment for your sin. We are already forgiven, and His grace has already restored you to His favor. There is nothing more that you need to do.

Day 2
The Grace of God: The Amazing Grace

Romans 5:1–11

Through whom also we have obtained our introduction by faith into this grace in which we stand.
Romans 5:5

Romans presents one of the greatest messages throughout Scripture. In chapter 5, Paul explains the depth of God's grace in that while we were still sinners, Christ died for us. For all the devastating results of sin, Christ provided the full and final remedy. When Adam and Eve first rebelled against God, sin entered the world, and as a result, death became engrained in the human experience. Even when God provided the law to teach us how to live, we further rebelled instead of responding in obedience. Yet, the more our sin increased, the more God's grace multiplied (v. 20). The result is a picture of God's grace that seems to border on the absurd. The more we acted out in rebellion against God, insisting that we go our way, the more God was moved with compassion and grace. Thus, the more we sin, the more Christ made His grace available to us.

Nevertheless, it is crucial to understand that the grace of God was not only realized at our salvation but also in the present as we live in the realm of God's grace. In verses 1–2, Paul states that we now have peace with God and a new relationship with Christ by grace. Furthermore, we now live permanently in the realm of His grace. In other words, we are forever enveloped and surrounded by His grace. This brings us joy and confidence even in the face of adversity. In a surprising statement, Paul uses the same word to describe the joy we have in the hope of glory (v. 2) and the joy he has even in the face of tribulations (v. 3). Because we are surrounded by God's favor and His deep concern for our helpless condition, we know that tribulations and trials are not a threat to our spiritual well-being. Because we reside in His grace, we stand securely regardless of the circumstances around us, for not only are we saved by His grace, but we are also kept secure by His grace. If Christ demonstrated His grace by reconciling us back to Him when we were His enemies, then how much more will He keep us by His grace now that we are in a loving relationship with Him.

The image presented in these verses is of God wrapping us in a protective bubble, so that no matter where we go or what we do or who we see, we have absolute assurance that we are completely protected from whatever threats surround us. When Paul states that we now stand in God's grace, he reminds us that in our relationship with Him, we have His protective grace surrounding us and guarding us so that our position with Him is secure even in the most trying of times. Such is the nature of His grace.

When you feel the pressure of today's struggles, remember that God's grace is enveloping you. When you are most desperate, God is most active. His grace assures you that He will not only wholly forgive your sins, but He will also respond to your needs in every moment. Such grace is truly amazing.

Day 3
The Mercy of God: God's Compassion for His People

Read Psalm 116

Gracious is the Lord, and righteous; yes, our God is compassionate. Psalm 116:5

It is one thing to know of others' suffering; it is quite another to be moved to take action to alleviate their suffering. Unfortunately, in an age of mass media, it is easy to become indifferent toward the distress of others. We watch the news and hear of some tragedy befalling people, and the next moment we change the channel to our favorite comedy show. While we may feel a momentary pain of sorrow for their tragedy, we quickly move on and forget the events as we become engrossed in the affairs of our own worlds. Only when the events touch us directly do we truly take notice. It is one thing to hear; it is quite another to listen genuinely.

The psalmist, in Psalm 116, knows the torment of intense trials. In verse 3, he is despairing of life itself. He presents a picture of being entirely and inescapably entangled by the rope of death. So deep is his distress that he sees no hope of rescue from the terrors surrounding him. However, just when it seems that his situation is hopeless, he turns to his last hope of deliverance: he cries out to God. This hope is not unfounded, but brings to his desperate mind a firm conviction that help is available. His hope is grounded in his belief that God does not just hear our cry, but He responds when we desperately call for help. The word picture presented by the phrase "He has inclined His ear to me" is that of a person who bends down and turns his ear toward the speaker to capture every word spoken. The term is often used in the literal sense of turning aside or diverting from the path that one is traveling. Thus, the picture is of God diverting from His way to carefully listen to our cries for help.

The psalmist does not give the basis for this confidence until verse 5. The reason he knows that God will respond stems from his understanding of God's compassion. This term refers to a deep love that results in the inward feeling of compassion, pity, and mercy. This word is also translated as *womb* and speaks of a mother's intense love and compassion for her nursing baby. One of the great imageries of love is the picture of a mother looking intently and lovingly at the baby nursing at her breast. Such is the image the Word paints for our understanding of God's mercy. When the term is used of God, it captures the depth of God's compassion and love for His children. When we speak of the mercy of God, we are identifying that aspect of God's character that has compassion on those in misery and distress. This is the confidence of the psalmist. In verse 15, we see the full extent of God's care when the psalmist states, "Precious in the sight of the LORD is the death of His godly ones." The idea is that when one of His children is at death's door, God is expressly watchful and attentive, making His presence known so that the person has comfort in death's hour. Likewise, when we are at our darkest hour of life, God is most attentive to us.

No matter what circumstances you face, whether they be occasions for joy or times of deep sorrow and fear, you can have the confidence that God's mercy is moving Him to act on your behalf. God is not indifferent or turning a deaf ear to your need; instead, He is attentive, watchful, and quickly turns aside to be with you and guide you when you are experiencing any trial in life. Therefore, when you are going through a time of sorrow, pain, or difficulty, be assured that God not only hears your prayer, but also that He truly listens intently, with a desire to act on your behalf.

Day 4
The Mercy of God: The Empathy of Christ

Read Hebrews 4:11–16

Let us draw near with confidence to the throne of grace, so that we may receive mercy and find grace to help in time of need. Hebrews 4:16

Our comfort in the struggles of life comes from those who do not merely sympathize with us, but genuinely empathize with what we are going through. Sympathy is a shared feeling, usually of sorrow, pity, or compassion for another person. Empathy, however, is more profound. It is the ability to put yourself in another's place and understand their feelings by identifying with them. Yet, even then, we have a sense that no one fully understands, for we are still individuals with diverse personalities, and we all process events differently. Thus, even when others have experienced similar struggles, they still do not fully understand what haunts our thoughts when sleep is fleeting in the middle of the night.

However, there is one who does fully understand. Christ did more than enter our world to bring salvation from sin. When He took on our human identity, He came to share our experiences and participate in all of life's triumphs and tragedies. He knew the sorrow of grief, the pain of rejection, the frustration of demands, the pangs of hunger, the exhaustion of sleeplessness, the struggles of temptation, and even the consequences of sin (not because He sinned, but because He took the results of our sin upon Himself). However, because He shares in our human experiences, He also knows and understands us even more than we do ourselves. He created us, formed our personalities, and shaped our identities, so He understands and knows how each of life's circumstances will affect us as individuals. Then, having shared our world, He entered heaven, not to leave us and abandon us, but to become our advocate who truly empathizes with us. He became our high priest, the one who provides the connecting point between us and God.

When we are going through trials and struggles, we are drawn to prayer. But our prayer is not merely the hopeful longing that God may see our condition and act on our behalf. We pray with confident expectation because we know that Christ is our advocate, standing in the Father's presence and assuring us that we can receive mercy and grace. In our weakness and sin, Christ bestows His grace (i.e., He will not pour out His punishment that we deserve) and His mercy (He sees our pitiful condition and responds to it). Consequently, we have the assurance that God will bring timely help to deal with the crisis we face. No matter the circumstance, whether the pressure of adversity, the pain of loss, or even the conflict with sin and temptation, we can honestly and openly come before God, knowing that He will not ignore or reject us but will genuinely empathize and respond to us.

The longer we deal with pressure, the more it weighs us down. It is one thing to face a week of the strain of uncertainty and apprehension; it is quite another when that week turns into months. The longer we feel the pressures of social isolation and uncertainty, the more we need to rely upon God and His strength. Then we can genuinely rediscover rest, for we know that God fully understands what we are experiencing, and He promises to give us the power we need to face the issues of this day.

Day 5
The Patience of God: Having One More Opportunity to Seek His Grace

Read 2 Peter 3:3–15

The Lord . . . is patient toward you, not wishing for any to perish but for all to come to repentance. 2 Peter 3:9

Patience is not a highly sought-after virtue in a fast-paced society desiring instant gratification. We get impatient when traffic is moving slowly. We become frustrated and irritable when people keep us waiting. We get annoyed when a restaurant is slow in serving our food. We even get impatient with God when He does not promptly deliver us from our trials.

While patience is often difficult for us, it is intrinsic to the goodness of God. In 2 Peter 3:9, Peter highlights that the delay in God's judgment is not because of some oversight on God's part but because of His desire to provide us every opportunity to respond to His grace and forgiveness. In Ezekiel 18, after pronouncing judgment upon those who reject Him, God gives an offer of hope. He assures us that a wicked man, no matter how great his sins, shall receive forgiveness if he turns from all his sin and surrenders in obedience to the will of God, for God has "no pleasure in the death of the wicked . . . rather that he should turn from his ways and live" (Ezekiel 18:23). For all our failures, God patiently withholds His justice to give us every opportunity to repent.

However, the declaration of God's patience also comes with a warning, for there will be those who see the delay in God's judgment as evidence that He will never judge (v. 4). So we become complacent, continuing to follow our lusts while blissfully ignoring the warnings. As time slowly marches on, we begin to think that time will continue "just as it was from the beginning of creation," even forgetting the judgment of God when He brought a universal flood upon the earth (v. 6). Thus, we abuse God's patience and use it as an excuse for our sin. We fail to recognize that a time will come when He destroys the heavens and earth with a consuming fire (vv. 7, 11–12).

This warning is not to paralyze us in fear but bring us to salvation. It is a reminder for us to be diligent in seeking Christ's redemption, for God does not take pleasure in the death of the wicked but desires all people to come to repentance. This again brings us back to the wonder of His grace and mercy. No matter how much we have ignored Him and His Word, insisting on our agenda every second we draw breath, we are reminded that He displays His patience and offers His grace one more time.

C. S. Lewis writes, "God whispers to us in our pleasures, speaks in our conscience, but shouts in our pains: it is His megaphone to rouse a deaf world . . . No doubt pain, as God's megaphone, is a terrible instrument; it may lead to final and unrepented rebellion. But it gives the only opportunity the bad man can have for amendment."[8] The trials we face today are not God's judgment, but they are His warning that His grace and mercy can be ignored only so long. While He is infinitely patient with us, He will not be eternally patient, for there will come a time when He executes His justice. Difficult times are a reminder that we are to seek the Lord while He may be found. So today, take an honest look at your life and make sure you are walking in fellowship with Him. His patience withholds His judgment so that you might embrace His grace.

---

8. C. S. Lewis, *The Problem of Pain* (New York: Macmillan Publishing Co., Inc, 1978).

The Holiness of God

He makes the clouds His chariot; He walks upon the
wings of the wind.

Psalm 104:3

A. W. Tozer wrote, "The greatness of God rouses fear within us, but His goodness encourages us not to be afraid of Him. To fear and not be afraid—that is the paradox of faith."[9] To fear God but lack confidence before God is to make sin inescapable and unforgivable. To have confidence before God without the fear of God is to make sin acceptable. The challenge today is that we no longer fear God. God has become a cosmic teddy bear who exists for our happiness but makes no demands upon our lives. Yet this perspective is not found in Scripture. In fact, the writers' attitudes were just the opposite. When individuals came face to face with God, their response was always the same—one of grave fear and a deep awareness of their sin (see Exodus 3:6, 20:18; Isaiah 6:5; Revelation 1:17). The proper fear of God is the beginning of wisdom (Proverbs 1:7) and serves as the foundation for obedience (Ecclesiastes 12:13). The lack of fear is a mark of the godless (Romans 3:13). To keep the balance between the fear of God and the confidence we have before Him, we must not only see

---

9. Tozer, 84.

His goodness, but we must also have a firm understanding of His holiness.

In John's vision of heaven in the book of Revelation, we see the curtain of heaven's throne room opened. In the majestic scene of God sitting upon the throne, the vision presented to us stands in sharp contrast to the casual, flippant attitude that we have toward God today. The picture is of a throne made from one large diamond embedded with fiery red rubies. Surrounding the throne is a rainbow that is emerald in color. The throne room presents us with a picture of God's glorious magnificence as well as His grace. Around the throne, we find twenty-four thrones, upon which sit twenty-four elders, joining the anthem of worship by casting their crowns before the Father in recognition that He sits in complete command over all rulers and authorities in heaven and earth. Proceeding from the throne are flashing lights and peals of thunder. In Isaiah 6, the sounds emanating from the throne room are so great that even the foundations of the thresholds tremble as the Seraphim proclaims the holiness of God. All of this serves to highlight God's glory and how He is distinct from all His creation in His absolute holiness.

The word "holy" means to be set apart, which, in the context of a relationship with God, speaks of God's holiness in two critical ways. First, it means that God is entirely separate from and transcendent above all things. There is none like Him, nor is there any equal to Him. This dispels any attempt we make to humanize God by bringing Him down to our level and making Him like us (albeit more significant and more powerful). It is utter folly to think that God is somehow answerable to us and that He should conform to our image and perspective. On the contrary, to affirm His holiness is to confirm His complete uniqueness.

Second, God's holiness refers to God's moral and ethical nature, that He is morally pure and utterly separate from anything that is morally evil. This not only means that He is without sin but also that He cannot be associated with anything or anyone tainted with sin. Furthermore, not only is He morally pure, but He defines what is morally right. This forces us to confront our often cavalier attitude toward sin. We make excuses; we take it lightly; we even think we can redefine it. We minimize its severity and ignore its consequences. However, this strikes against the very holiness of God. Because of His holiness, God views all sin, no matter how small and insignificant to us, as an absolute insult to His character.

Considering His holiness, there are two essential responses we must make. First, we must bow in humble worship of God. To worship God is to place value and worth upon Him. The word *glory* refers to that which is of great weight; in contrast is *vanity*, which speaks of a weightless, vaporless cloud. To use God's name in vain is to treat God and His person as that which has no weight or value. To take God's name in vain is not merely to use His title flippantly, but to make Him unimportant in our life, to place Him secondary to everything else in life.

The second response is one of submission. We reveal our attitude toward the holiness of God by surrendering to His supremacy and rule in our life. While we are invited into a personal relationship with God, it is essential to understand that it is not a relationship of equality. Instead, it is grounded in complete surrender to His will—to come to grips with the fact that He is God, and we are not. We cannot question Him; we can only submit to Him.

Day 1
The Holiness of God: His Unfathomable Holiness

Read Isaiah 6:1–7

Holy, Holy, Holy, is the LORD *of Hosts.* Isaiah 6:3

We cannot comprehend God's holiness. It is one of His attributes that we have no comparison for in our own existence. Intrinsic in God's holiness is the reality that He is wholly untouched and separate from all that is evil. It is not just that God is morally good, but that He is entirely separate from all that is tainted by sin. Therein lies our challenge. Because we are sinful by birth and choice, we cannot envision being free from its effect and presence. Instead of being repulsed by sin, we tolerate it and accept it. Whereas God, in His holiness, finds sin offensive and abhorrent, we find it pleasurable and agreeable. In a fallen world where our sinful nature taints everything we do, experience, desire, and think, we can't comprehend what it is like to be genuinely holy. The very fact that we find sin tolerable and desirable reveals how little we understand what holiness is.

It is not without significance that when the heavenly host sings the song of God's praise, they focus on His holiness. His unmitigated holiness serves to encompass the totality of God's attributes and His being. While we would sing the song of His love and grace, the angels proclaim His holiness. If God were not holy, He would no longer be good, loving, just, righteous, and perfect. Instead, He would be an evil and capricious tyrant to be feared rather than worshiped. Thus, God's holiness is not just one attribute among many; it serves to describe the inherent nature of all His attributes. He is not only a loving God; He possesses a holy love. He is not merely a gracious God; His grace is holy, untainted by the effects of sin. His perfection puts God in a class all by Himself, for the gods of our creation are inevitably tainted by sin.

Not only is the holiness of God challenging for us to grasp, but it is also His one attribute that we often ignore. To be confronted with His holiness is to be confronted with our sinfulness. Consequently, we desire to bring God down to our level, to conform God to our image in order to make ourselves more like God, elevating ourselves to be equal with God, and enabling ourselves to live independently of Him. However, in creating "God" in our image, we inevitably project our sinful nature upon Him and His moral standard. What God finds repugnant, we label as acceptable.

This week, as we contemplate the holiness of God, we must begin with a humble recognition of how impossible it is for us to understand what it genuinely means. We must set aside our sense of self-righteousness and self-determination of right and wrong, and instead, in complete humility, ask God to give us an expanded vision of His holiness. So today, set aside all of your perceptions of God and ask Him to provide you with a new and fresh view of His holiness.

Day 2
The Holiness of God: Recognizing His Uniqueness

Read Isaiah 44:1–8

I am the first, and I am the last, and there is no God besides Me. Isaiah 44:6

The people of Israel in the time of Isaiah were no different than our society today. Instead of exclusively worshiping God, they had fallen into spiritual and religious syncretism. Rather than worshiping God alone, they had adopted and accepted the beliefs of the various religions surrounding them. There is little difference between what they did and what we see today in our modern view of religion. Today, it is prevalent for people to adopt different religious perspectives, accepting all religions as equally viable ways to find God. It is not uncommon for people to share quotes on Facebook from Hinduism, Buddhism, and the Bible as if all were sources of divine knowledge and wisdom.

In contrast, Isaiah calls people to the awareness that God is unique, that there is no other God but Him. Central to the biblical understanding of holiness is the uniqueness of God—that He is separate from all other gods. The Hebrew word for holy (*qadosh*) means to be marked off or separate. To affirm that God is holy is to confirm that there is no one like Him and that He does not share His glory with anyone. Therefore, it is not surprising that we find statements affirming God's uniqueness six times in chapters 40–46. God is not simply greater than the other gods, but there is truly no other god except for Him. To worship any other god, or even to acknowledge the existence of any other god, is ultimately to deny God's holiness and majesty. In Isaiah 44:7, we are challenged to identify any being or religion that can match God's sovereign and unique claims. There is none, for all other gods are merely idols created by man and are useless (vv. 9–20). For the writers of Scripture, the idea that God could be compared to any other god (or man) is utterly unthinkable and blasphemous, for it undermines His character.

The holiness of God is not just theological jargon but the foundation of our hope amid the struggles we face in life, including our battle with sin. Because He is unique and unparalleled, He is the only one who brings salvation from our troubles (43:11). If we place our complete trust and faith in Him, then we can have confidence, for our God is the only one who can truly save us. To seek salvation and help from any other god will ultimately bring disappointment, for they are ultimately a myth, a product of our imagination. Because God is holy, we do not need to be fearful or dismayed. He alone is our Rock. The imagery of God as a rock provides a picture of God as a place of security, a place of protection from attack, a place of safety amidst the storms of life. Since there is no other Rock but God, He alone is the only one who deserves our trust, and He alone is the one who will bring us true deliverance.

If you feel the pressure of the day and the discouragement and helplessness that comes when adversity threatens your well-being, turn to the only one who is genuinely holy, unique, and transcendent over all else. He alone is God, and He alone is the one who is willing and able to bring hope and salvation. He alone is holy.

Day 3
The Holiness of God: His Moral Purity

Read Habakkuk 1:12–17

Your eyes are too pure to approve evil. Habakkuk 1:13

Our sin nature makes it impossible for us to grasp God's absolute moral purity and holiness. No matter how much we may discuss it, no matter how many books we may read about it, no matter how many hours we spend contemplating its significance, in the end, we still project upon God our moral corruptness. This is especially true when we are going through times of extreme difficulty and sorrow. When confronted with the tragedy and the confusion of life, we cannot help but question God's motives and actions. Since we fail in our lives so frequently, we begin to question God's goodness when our experience seems to contradict it.

Such was the case of the prophet Habakkuk. In Habakkuk 1:12–13, he gives us a profound statement and insight into the nature of God's holiness. When he speak of God's holiness, he affirm that God is untouched, unaffected, and utterly separate from moral impurity. So pure and holy is God that He cannot look upon it, nor does He ever approve it. It is not just that God Himself can do no moral wrong, but that God cannot be associated with anything or anyone immoral or impure.

God's separation from sin causes Habakkuk's confusion. As Habakkuk looked around him and saw the triumph of the wicked, he began to question God's holiness (v. 13b). How can a holy God remain silent when the wicked seem to win the day? Heaven appeared to be silent and indifferent when the idolatrous Chaldeans were conquering Israel. If God is holy, then how can He not act when evil nations attack His chosen people? We wrestle with the same question when we face suffering and trials in our lives. Why do we suffer when others, who reject God and His Word, seem to suffer no hardships in their lives? How can God be holy and tolerate sin?

In chapter 2, God provides the answer. He does notice, and He will act, for He is holy; therefore, let all the earth be silent. God will vindicate His holiness and bring judgment upon sin, but it will be in His timing and according to His purposes. In the end, Habakkuk is silenced before a God who sits upon His holy throne, untouched by sin. Instead of allowing circumstances to drive our faith, Habakkuk learned that faith must govern his understanding of God (2:4). When Habakkuk realigns his faith to trust in the holy God rather than judge God by his experiences, then he affirms, "I will exult in the LORD, I will rejoice in the God of my salvation. The Lord God is my strength, and He has made my feet like hind's feet and makes me walk on my high places" (Habakkuk 3:18–19).

God's absolute perfection provides us with perspective on life's circumstances. When we are discouraged, facing insurmountable struggles, or overwhelmed by circumstances surrounding us, it is easy for us to start to question God. Because we are marred by sin, we begin to question the moral purity of God and the moral purity of His motives and actions. We start to wonder if God is as inherently flawed as we are. This is when we must realign our perspective by our faith in God and His Word. Faith enables us to affirm and trust that God is intrinsically pure; therefore, all His actions and motives are pure. In the end, we can simply rest in Him, not because we have deliverance from our circumstances, but because we know that God is pure and holy, and He will always act on our behalf, with our best interests in mind, in such a way that brings Him glory.

Day 4
The Holiness of God: Finding Holiness Through Suffering

Read Exodus 15:1–18

Who is like You, majestic in holiness . . . in Your strength You have guided them to Your holy habitation. Exodus 15:11

Just when it seemed God had rescued the people of Israel from the clutches of slavery, the situation took a dramatic turn for the worse. After Pharaoh let the people go, he changed his heart, gathered his formidable army, and aggressively pursued them into the empty wilderness. The Israelites were trapped: in front of them, an impassable body of water; behind, the Pharaoh and his horses and chariots (the ancient equivalent of tanks), bent on revenge. It is little wonder that the people became frightened and began to doubt Moses's and God's purposes. However, what causes panic and despair in our hearts is no threat to an infinitely powerful God who is majestic in His Holiness.

In a powerful display of God's power over creation, the nations, and the affairs of man, God spectacularly acted on behalf of the Israelites. First, He positioned His mighty angel, who was serving as their protective guide, to stand between Egypt's armies and the people of Israel, serving as an impassable defensive wall between them. Then He sent a strong wind, causing the waters to separate and enabling the people to cross the sea. So thorough was God's deliverance that the text mentions that they crossed on *dry* land. They did not even have to march through the typical mud that sits on the bottom of any body of water. However, even as they crossed, the Egyptians were not deterred but pursued after them. Finally, God destroyed their army and put Pharaoh to death when He brought the waters crashing down upon them in a dramatic and final defeat of Egypt,. This defeat was so devastating it would be centuries before Egypt would again become a dominant nation in the Ancient Near East. While the people cowered in fear that God's plans were going awry, God was working to reveal His holiness and guide the people, not only to the land He had promised them but to the dwelling place of God's protection. The word translated *habitation* (v. 13) refers to the enclosure of a shepherd where he provides safety and security for the sheep. When the term is used in connection with God, it speaks of the place where God protects His people, culminating in the eschatological dwelling of God's people—i.e., the messianic city.

As the pressures mount around us, our focus naturally shifts from God's activity to our own crises. As a result, we, like the people of Israel, begin to question God's plan and doubt God's continual care. However, God uses suffering and adversity to reveal His holiness and guide us to His dwelling place. Suffering is not a threat to us; instead, it is used by God to demonstrate His holiness, that He is unique and unparalleled, and that He alone is God. When we encounter situations beyond our ability to control, we begin to understand and appreciate God's holiness. What we see as threats become opportunities for us to see God in a new and fresh way. When you start to feel discouraged, insecure, or threatened, prayerfully ask God for a new and fresh understanding of Him. Ask God to reveal His awesome holiness and then trust that He can do something incredible in your life, not necessarily by altering your circumstances but by transforming your view of Him.

Day 5
The Holiness of God: Being Holy in Purity and Service

Read Leviticus 11:41–47

Consecrate yourselves, therefore, and be holy, for I am holy. Leviticus 11:44

The book of Leviticus remains an enigma for the casual reader, filled with guidelines prescribing how the people were to conduct themselves in various scenarios. To the modern reader, the book seems confusing and outdated. However, a closer reading reveals several factors behind the dietary laws and the clean/

unclean laws. First, many nutritional regulations were designed to protect the people in an age when cooking practices did not always provide proper protection from food-borne pathogens. Second, many of the statutes responded to the pagan worship practices surrounding the people of Israel. Thus, regulations were established to keep Israel from embracing the idolatry of these various false religions. For example, the laws of motherhood in chapter 12 provided a safeguard for Israel from the fertility rites common in the pagan religions by separating childbirth from religious worship. However, the most crucial key to understanding the book, which served to govern all rules and regulations, is found in Exodus 11:45. The call to be holy even as God is holy is at the center of all of the Old Testament laws, regulations, and ethical commands.

God's holiness is not just at the center of the Old Testament moral and ethical code, but also at the heart of the New Testament. The standard to which God calls us is one of personal holiness. Just as God's holiness means that He is entirely separate from His creation, so He calls us to be distinct in conduct and morality from the world in which we live. Paul points to this when he writes, "Do not be conformed to this world but be transformed by the renewing of your mind, so that you may prove what the will of God is." (Romans 12:2). To be holy means that our standard of moral conduct should not be determined by the world in which we live but by the holiness and character of God.

Furthermore, holiness deals with our relationship with God. To be holy is to be set apart for God's use and glory; it is to be devoted to serving God so that our relationship with Him governs everything we do. In Leviticus, we find that the utensils used in the temple were declared to be holy. A bowl was declared holy and could only be used in the temple for God's worship and was no longer to be used for any common purpose. When God pronounces that we are to be holy, he is not only calling us to ethical and moral holiness; he is calling us to be wholly devoted to serving Him. This is the point that Paul is making in Romans 12:1: "Therefore I urge you, brethren, by the mercies of God, to present your bodies a living and holy sacrifice, acceptable to God, which is your spiritual service of worship."

This is what brings us clarity in a confusing world. As we go through the upheavals of life, our first thought is, "How can I get back to a normal life?" However, this misses the point of God's calling. Instead, the question should be, "How can I serve God effectively during this time of uncertainty?" This is the calling of the Christian. We are not called to a life of our choosing and a life of ease. We are called to be devoted to God. Instead of getting caught up in all the turmoil of the day, focus on looking for opportunities to serve.

The Righteousness of God

The Rock! His work is perfect, for all His ways are just; a God of faithfulness and without injustice, righteous and upright is He.

Deuteronomy 32:4

W e live in an age of the smorgasbord religion and the smorgasbord God. Smorgasbords are the perfect place to take a group of people: you go down the line and pick and choose what you want and pass over what you do not. Tragically, today we approach our faith and our view of God as though we can individualize Christianity to our liking. We go down the ecclesiastical smorgasbord to the meat and potatoes of discipleship. Then we go to the dessert table and load up grace and love. But then we come to the table that everyone skips, the table filled with the righteousness of God and His wrath toward sin.

In our worship, we celebrate the mercy and grace of God. We sing of His presence and wisdom. His power overwhelms us. We even proclaim His holiness. Yet rarely do we rejoice in His justice and wrath. However, just as God is glorified in His love and compassion, so also is His glory revealed in His justice, righteousness, and judgment. Ezekiel proclaims,

> *Thus says the* LORD *God, "Behold, I am against you,*
> *O Sidon, and I will be glorified in your midst. Then*
> *they will know that I am the* LORD *when I execute*
> *judgments in her, and I will manifest My holiness in*
> *her. For I will send pestilence to her and blood to her*
> *streets, and the wounded will fall in her midst by the*
> *sword upon her on every side; then they will know*
> *that I am the* LORD." *(Ezekiel 28:22)*

To worship God, we must worship Him in His totality, not in a piecemeal fashion where we pick and choose certain qualities.

It is not surprising that the psalmist in Psalm 11 provides a celebration of righteousness and justice. In light of the triumph of the wicked and the fear they bring, he finds his hope in the justice of God. When we speak of the righteousness of God, we are affirming that God always acts in accord with what is right and that His character determines what is right. In other words, God is the standard of what is right, and He always acts in conformity to that standard. God is infinitely righteous in His being and all that He does. He governs the universe in righteousness. Unfortunately, we live in an age where right and wrong have become fluid without any objective standard. In this age, we need to go back to the foundational truth that God's character and nature—and not humanity—determine right and wrong.

This brings us to the justice of God. His righteousness speaks of the truth that He always acts according to His law and responds to humanity based upon His standard. Law without justice (the reward for those who obey or punishment for those who disobey) ultimately promotes unrighteousness. If God does not punish sin, He tolerates sin, which makes Him sinful. As the ruler of the universe, there is nothing that escapes His notice. Consequently, He tests the hearts of people and brings judgment upon sin.

While we see His justice as something to fear, for the psalmist, it becomes the foundation of hope. Sin and evil do not win the day, for there comes a time when God will bring judgment upon sin and bring an end to corruption. However, even as He executes the severity of His judgment, He offers hope and salvation for the worst sinner who accepts His grace. For in His grace, He provided a substitute, one who would fulfill the righteous standard of God and His requirement for the punishment of sin by taking the judgment we merit and placing it upon Himself. The person who provided the judicial satisfaction of God's justice was Christ via His death on the cross. If we accept His salvation, then we are now declared righteous before God. Just as His justice warns of the judgment of sin, His justice also guarantees our freedom when His justice is satisfied. It is because God is just that we know He will not go back upon His word. If we have accepted Christ, we have the assurance that we are now in right standing before God and have eternal life. For this very reason, His justice is worthy of our praise.

Day 1
The Righteousness of God: The Standard of Right and Wrong

Read Psalm 33

He loves righteousness and justice. Psalm 33:5

For years, the determination for weights and measurements was arbitrary at best. For example, when someone purchased milk from a local farmer, there was an *implied* definition of the measurement. However, there was no *consistent* definition. How people would measure a gallon of milk in one area might be radically different from how they would determine a gallon in another. It was not until Louis A. Fischer, chief of the Metrology Division of the National Bureau of Standards, published a paper in the First Annual Meeting of the Scalers of Weights and Measurements that a recognized standard for determining weights and measurements was established. Because of the influence of his paper, he became known as the father of modern weights and measurements today.

While Louis A. Fischer established the foundation for a consistent standard of weights and measurements, we are faced with a more critical question today. We live in a time when morality and the definition of right and wrong are continuously and radically shifting. In the last thirty years, our culture has seen a dramatic shift in defining right and wrong. What was once taboo thirty years ago is now regarded as acceptable and usual. Today, some of the most popular shows on cable TV display content previously considered softcore pornography, available only in seedy adult bookstores. In today's upside-down world, wrong has become right, and right has become wrong.

Is there a standard for right and wrong in this age of moral chaos, or is morality determined merely by the latest polls or the tweet of the most popular "social influencer"? The answer is not grounded in the evolving opinions of people but in the eternal and unchanging character of God. In Psalm 33, the psalmist invites us to join him in a musical anthem of praise to God, who loves righteousness and justice. Not that God just upholds the standard of righteousness; He *is* righteousness. In other words, He is the standard of right and wrong. By Him, all morality is measured and governed.

God is not only the source and standard of righteousness; He always acts according to what is right. When we face the struggles of life and encounter harrowing experiences, we can begin to question God's righteousness. How can He be righteous and just when heaven seems silent in response to the suffering of the innocent? Why does God not act on our behalf? These are not just hypothetical questions but ones that shake the very foundation of our faith. This brings us back to the heart of faith and trust in God. Because righteousness is intrinsic to His nature, we have the assurance that God always acts in accordance with what is right. His character is righteous, so it follows that He is always blameless in both His plans and their execution. We may not fully understand it now, but we know that His perspective, which is often different from ours, is perfect and right, and His actions are always correct and in conformity with His character. Faith is not the ability to always see God's purpose and plan, but the ability to trust Him even while we cannot see. Faith is living with the knowledge that God always does what is right even when it seems wrong from our perspective. This week, as you feel the pressures of the day and find yourself questioning God, offer up an anthem of praise that He is righteous, and so His actions are always correct and proper.

Day 2
The Righteousness of God: Resting in Him

Read Job 40:1–9

Will you really annul My judgment? Will you condemn Me that you may be justified? Job 40:8

Within the pain of his tragedy, Job was facing a crisis of faith. He had been faithful in his obedience to God, but in a cruel act of injustice (from Job's perspective), it seemed as if God had turned against him. It is one thing to suffer when it is a consequence of our sin and choices, but it is quite another when our suffering seems arbitrary, unjust, and without cause or reason. That was what was causing Job to struggle in his faith. Even his friends turned against him, accusing him of concealing his sin and refusing to acknowledge his guilt. For them, there was an inevitable link between suffering and evil. In the three friends' minds, the reason we suffer is because God is bringing His judgment upon our rebellion. But deep down, Job knew that was not the case. Job was not being self-righteous, becoming blind to his weaknesses. While not seeing himself as perfect, he could not reconcile the severity of his suffering with the integrity of his life. As he affirms in chapter 31, he had lived his life in obedience to God's law, and when he failed, he responded with confession and repentance.

After the extended silence from heaven during which the three friends made their accusations against Job, God finally broke His silence and answered Job. However, the answer was both surprising and unexpected. From the outside, the reader is given insight that Job and his three friends were not privy to— namely, that Job was not suffering because of any sin; he was suffering because of his righteousness. Consequently, when God does speak, we expect God to explain, to share with Job what we already know to be accurate—that Job is righteous, and God was using this struggle to reveal the actual depth of Job's character. Yet, in a surprising turn, God does not answer Job's questions or explain why Job is suffering. Instead, God points out that He alone is righteous and just. God reminds Job that we cannot contend with God or accuse God of injustice, for we are inherently flawed. God does not need to explain or justify His actions, for He is the Creator, and He is the one who determines justice. Who are we to ascribe injustice to God or override His judgment (v. 8)? Our folly is revealed when we think that God needs to justify His actions to us. We need to come to accept that God does not have to explain His actions. He is not obligated to win our approval. Instead, we are to submit to Him in faith.

When we experience deep pain and suffering, it is easy to begin to question God's actions, to feel unjustly treated by God. But when we do so, we are making God corrupt. Since God is the final standard of righteousness, we can trust Him to do what is right even though it is not apparent. God will never act contrary to the moral law He has established. He will "always do right by us." Therefore, to question Him is to suspect His very divine character. Rather than becoming ensnared with doubting God, we need to simply rest in our trust in Him, knowing that He has a different perspective and that His actions are always right. In the end, all we can do is admit with Job that "I am insignificant; what can I reply to you? I lay my hand on my mouth" (v. 4). This enables us to rest in our confidence in His righteousness even when we do not understand why He allows us to face the circumstances we confront.

Day 3
The Justice of God: Finding True Justice in an Unjust World

2 Thessalonians 1:5–8; Psalm 73:1–13

It is only just for God to repay. 2 Thessalonians 1:6

In society today there is a clamor for justice. When people use their personal power or the law to abuse others' rights, we rightfully demand that justice be enforced. When we feel that we or others have been wrongfully mistreated, we call for justice. But, under the guise of fairness, when people disregard the law themselves, we become enraged, for any distortion of justice ultimately promotes evil.

As we have previously seen, God is righteousness in the word's most authentic and purest sense. God is not merely one who acts righteously; He is the definition of righteousness. However, essential to all righteousness is the upholding of that standard. An unjust person is not only one who breaks the law but who also refuses to uphold the law and enforce the consequences when the law is broken. This is especially true of God's law. Therefore, when we speak of God's justice, we refer to the fact that He acts in conformity with His law, and He administers His kingdom by that law by bringing punishment to the wicked and rewards to the righteous.

In 2 Thessalonians 1, Paul is addressing those who are facing persecution and affliction because of their faith. When this happens, people can become discouraged and question God's justice. However, Paul reminds them that the righteousness of God leads to the justice of God. While His integrity establishes the moral laws of the universe, His justice treats people according to the requirements of the law and their response to His law. He brings rewards to those who obey and retribution to those who break His moral law. As the church at Thessalonica was facing persecution and suffering, it would have been easy for them to begin to question the justice of God, for it seemed as if their oppressors remained unjudged. But Paul points out that there would come a time when God executed His justice, and those persecuting the church would be repaid for their actions. God will bring retributions to those who reject Christ and refuse to obey God's commands (v. 8–9), but He will also reward the righteous for their obedience (v. 10). In the end, justice will prevail.

As we look at the world, it is easy to conclude that wickedness wins the day, and righteousness is ignored. Like the psalmist, we can cry out, "Behold, these are the wicked; and always at ease, they have increased in wealth. Surely in vain I have kept my heart pure and washed my hands in innocence" (Psalm 73:12–13). As a result, we can begin to stumble in our faith (v. 2). Yet, there is hope. No matter how much we see injustice in our world today, God will, in His perfect time, bring His justice that is perfect, impartial, and grounded in His moral law. We do not need to get discouraged when we face adversity and inequality in the world, for these will continue to remain as long as sin remains. Instead, we can anticipate the day when God will execute His justice upon those who reject His law, and give rewards to those who believe and follow Him (v. 10). When He comes to establish His kingdom, He will reign in perfect righteousness and execute perfect justice. Wrong will no longer be regarded as right, and evil will no longer be able to run rampant without any punishment. While we see the injustice in the world and the apparent injustice in our suffering, we can find comfort knowing that there will come a time when God sets all things right.

Day 4
The Righteousness of God and His Wrath: The Holy Response of Justice

Read Nahum 1:2–9

Who can stand before His indignation? Who can endure the burning of His anger? Nahum 1:6

The title of the sermon that day in Enfield, Connecticut, would hardly be popular today. The text for the message was found in

Deuteronomy 32:35: "Vengeance is Mine, and retribution. In due time their foot will slip; for the day of their calamity is near, and the impending things are hastening upon them." In this sermon, the preacher would confront the sinner with the inevitable wrath of God: "The wrath of God burns against them, their damnation does not slumber; the pit is prepared, the fire is made ready, the furnace is now hot, ready to receive them; the flames do now rage and glow. The glittering sword is whet and held over them, and the pit hath opened its mouth under them." He would conclude that day with this invitation: "Therefore, let every one that is out of Christ, now awake and fly from the wrath to come. The wrath of Almighty God is now undoubtedly hanging over a great part of this congregation. Let everyone fly out of Sodom: 'Haste and escape for your lives, look not behind you, escape to the mountain, lest you be consumed.'"[10]

The message preached that day would profoundly affect the listeners and result in one of the greatest revivals in our nation. The preacher was Jonathan Edwards, and the title of the message, one that would be ignored today, was "Sinners in the Hands of an Angry God." In a world where we want a God who accepts all people regardless of their religious beliefs, lifestyle, or behavior, we have forgotten that intrinsic in the nature of God is His wrath. It should not escape our notice that God's wrath is mentioned more frequently in Scripture than His love.

This is what Nahum reminds us of in his message, that the wrath of God should never be dismissed or taken lightly. When God's anger bursts forth against sin, even the foundations of the earth quake in His presence (v. 5). When we speak of the righteousness and justice of God, we must in the same breath affirm His holy indignation and anger at sin. When we mention the wrath of God, we are not talking about the explosive fury of a spoiled child who did not get his way. Instead, we are referring to

10. Jonathan Edwards, *Legacy of Faith Library: Works of Jonathan Edwards* (Nashville: B&H Publishing Group), 57–78.

His deep and intense hatred of all sin. It is judicial wrath poured out on those who have rejected righteousness and, in so doing, have chosen for themselves the judgment of God (for the New Testament equivalent, see John 3:16–19, 36).

However, in the terror-striking outpouring of God's anger, we find a ray of hope, for, amid the description of the terrible wrath of God, we see the offer of hope and protection for those who trust in Him. In verse 7, we read, "The LORD is good, a stronghold in the day of trouble, and He knows those who take refuge in him." Our greatest terror is to stand in the presence of a holy God who, in the outworking of His justice, pours out His wrath upon our sin. However, the greatest joy is to have that wrath averted to the person of Christ, who paid the penalty for our sin so that we might experience His grace. Today, the suffering we face serves as a reminder that sin needs a remedy, which is found only in Christ. Our acceptance or rejection of that message will determine whether we experience His wrath or grace. If we have accepted Christ's offer of salvation, then we find hope in our present suffering, for the joys of heaven await us because of God's grace. If we have rejected the offer of salvation, our greatest joys in the present are empty, for, in the end, there only awaits the eternal wrath of God. The choice is now yours to make.

Day 5
The Righteousness of God: The Hope of Salvation

Read Romans 3:21–28

The righteousness of God through faith in Jesus Christ for all those who believe. Romans 3:22

The most perplexing question confronting us in our understanding of God's character and nature is not, "How can a loving God judge sinners?" Instead, the problem that defies human explanation is, "How can a just and righteous God accept sinners?" If we are truly honest with ourselves (and often we are not), we must admit that we are sinners by both nature and action. To truly understand the righteousness of God is to be powerfully confronted with how far we fall short in attaining His standard. There is not a day that goes by in which we do not violate and disregard His standard of right and wrong. When we stand before God, we will do so without excuse. We have chosen, and continually decided, to go our own way and reject God.

Consequently, all of us stand before God as guilty, as breakers of His law, and, as a result, we are deserving of His wrath (Romans 3:23). While we want to trivialize sin and categorize sin according to some degree of severity, we fail to recognize that all sin, however minor in our eyes, is an affront to the holiness of God and a complete rejection of His law. To break one of His laws is to violate all His laws. This brings us to the inevitable consequence we must face: that we are all sinners worthy of judgment. Thus, we are confronted again with the question, "How can a just and righteous God accept us as sinners?"

This is the question Paul is asking in this passage. Since we are all sinners who fall short of the glory of God, how can we be saved? Indeed, salvation is not through our own righteousness and obedience to the law, for we have all rebelled against God and stand guilty in His presence. The more we attempt to earn our salvation through our own efforts, the more we reveal how far short we come (vv. 19–20). The answer to our great dilemma is found in Christ. Christ became the propitiation for our sin. The word *propitiation* refers to the reality that Christ became our substitute when He bore the infinite wrath of God for our sin so that, instead of being the objects of God's wrath, we are now the objects of His favor. The result is that we can no longer boast in our abilities or powers; rather, we can boast only in the work of Christ. In other words, Christ accomplishes what we could never achieve for ourselves. We are no longer regarded as guilty before God; instead, we are now declared innocent by His actions. In His death, He took upon Himself the penalty for all our sins in the past, present, and future, so now we are not only free from the penalty of sin, but we are also elevated to the position of being children of God.

This brings us back to the question: if we have rejected Him, rebelled against His law, and so are now objects of His wrath, why would He ever be moved to offer us not only salvation but also position of being His loved children, who are now co-heirs with Christ? No wonder that after contemplating the complete work of Christ on our behalf in Romans 1–11, Paul concludes by stating, "O, the depth of the riches both of the wisdom and knowledge of God! How unsearchable are His judgments and unfathomable His ways!" (Romans 11:33). If we do not marvel at His grace toward us, then we do not grasp the severity of our sin and the splendor of His righteousness. When we are going through trials, it is easy to question God's goodness and grace. However, all we must do is look back at the cross to realize that the extent of God's grace toward us is indeed immeasurable. We may not understand what He is doing now in the midst of our trials, but we can find joy in what He has already done.

The Faithfulness of God

For you light my lamp; the Lord my God illumines my darkness.

Psalm 18:28

I n an age of mass information, we have become cynical regarding truth. Politicians give guarantees they have no intention of keeping in order to obtain our votes. In the advertising industry, companies make claims about their products that inevitably fall short. Couples stand before an officiant to make a lifelong pledge of their love, only to break those promises in a few years when the going gets tough. Truth has become relative, and faithfulness to one's commitment has become empty words. Because we are unfaithful to our promises, we assume God is not faithful to his. We sometimes approach the Scriptures with the same suspicion as we approach the news.

However, our hope and salvation are grounded in the faithfulness of God, that His Word is always accurate, and His promise is always valid. To affirm the faithfulness of God is to confirm that His Word and promises are just as relevant and binding today as they were when He first spoke to them over two thousand years ago. When we open the pages of Scripture, we discover that God's faithfulness is grounded in His redemptive purposes. In Genesis 17:1–8, God made a covenant with Abraham to make His descendants into a great nation. He promised to bless them and to be their God. This covenant was reaffirmed in the Mosaic covenant. Still, the generation that stood on the foot of Mt. Sinai did not enjoy the benefits of the covenant because they rejected God in their unbelief. As a result, for forty years, they wandered in the wilderness until a new generation arose. It was this generation that then stood on the borders of the promised land. In Deuteronomy, as they were poised to enter the land, God not only reaffirmed His covenant, but He reminded them that they were to be a holy people, set apart for God (Deuteronomy 7:6). Peter applies this same verse to us (1 Peter 2:9), pointing to God's redemptive purpose throughout history. This purpose involves our salvation from the bondage of sin and being called to be a people of God's possession. This redemptive purpose is not based upon our intrinsic value or worth but solely upon God's grace (Deuteronomy 7:7–8). Just as God loved Israel even though they were the smallest of nations, He also loves us, who are least deserving of His favor.

After understanding God's love and redemptive purpose for us, we find that the basis for our confidence in His promise is grounded in His faithfulness. Thus, Moses reminds the people, and us today, "Know therefore that the LORD your God, He is God, the faithful God, who keeps His covenant and His loving-kindness to a thousandth generation with those who love Him and keep His commandments; but repays those who hate Him to their faces, to destroy them; He will not delay with him who hates Him, He will repay him to his face" (Deuteronomy 7:9–10). To speak of His faithfulness is to affirm that God is always dependable, sure, and faithful to His word. He does not waffle on His promises. God does not backtrack. He does not renege on His promise. Every promise God makes is sure and dependable because He is a God who is reliable and trustworthy. The statement that He keeps His covenant to a thousandth generation is a hyperbolic statement meaning that He can be counted upon always and forever. Approximately one out of every four verses in the Bible contains a specific promise. Here are some of the most important promises He has made to us:

- The promise of salvation: "That whoever believes in Him shall not perish but have eternal life" (John 3:16)
- The promise of Christ's abiding presence: "I am with you always to the ends of the earth" (Matthew 28:19)
- The promise of the indwelling presence of His Spirit to guide us in the truth (John 14:26)
- The promise that He will protect us from temptation (1 Corinthians 10:13)
- The promise that He will love us unconditionally (Romans 8:38–39)
- The promise that we will be co-heirs with Christ (Romans 8:17)
- The promise that He will answer our prayers (Matthew 7:7–11)
- The promise that He upholds and protects us during the deepest trials of life (Psalm 23)
- The promise that we will share in His divine nature (2 Peter. 1:4)
- The promise that God will provide for all our needs (Philippians 4:19)

We have the confidence that He will fulfill each of these promises because God is always trustworthy. When you read a promise God has given, it is an oath you can completely count on to be true. Even when we fail, God remains devoted to His word.

When we are going through difficult times, it is easy to allow our circumstances to create doubt in God's word. There are times when it seems as if our experience contradicts what He has stated. God is faithful and true; therefore, we know that He will always be proven right in the end. When you need hope, do not look to your circumstances. Look to the character of God.

Day 1
The Faithfulness of God: The Assurance of Our Security

Read Psalm 91:1–16

His faithfulness is a shield and bulwark. Psalm 91:4

Psalm 91 is written for times of uncertainty in the face of grave perils. In verses 5–12, we see an array of circumstances that bring real threats and overwhelming fear. First, we see the onslaught of pestilence, disease, and illness (vv. 3, 6, 10). Second, we hear the approaching footprints of enemies bringing destructive war (vv. 3, 5, 7). Third, we feel the apprehension of a traveler walking alone on a dangerous path (vv. 12–13). Finally, we experience the terror that comes when surrounded by unseen threats in the darkness of night (v. 5). These serve to provide us with a picture of the circumstances that create overwhelming anxiety. They are outside our control and beyond our ability to overcome.

But unlike the psalms of lament (such as Psalm 13), where the psalmist feels abandoned by God, this psalmist writes from the context of confidence and assurance that God will be present and active in our lives, protecting us from all the threats we face. When we dwell in the shelter of the Most High, we discover a place of absolute security and impenetrable protection (vv. 1–2). This response is not merely offering up a quick prayer, asking for God's protective hand when things start getting rough. Instead, the terms *dwell* and *abide* point to making one's residence in and continuing to live in the presence of God. Our God often seems distant in times of trials because we only seek Him when problems come. Instead of seeing the presence of God as a place to live permanently, we only see Him as a fortress to flee to when pressures mount. However, the rest of the time, we go our separate ways, living life as if He doesn't exist, or at least has little involvement in our lives.

When we center our lives on our relationship with God, we begin to see life differently. We know that He is indeed the one we can rely upon in all circumstances because He is eternally faithful. To affirm His faithfulness is to confirm that He is wholly and always dependable. God's faithfulness means that He is always trustworthy and committed to His word and that He fulfills every promise He makes.

God's fidelity becomes our "shield and bulwark" (Psalm 91:4). The term *shield* refers to the full-length protecting shield the soldiers stood behind in battle to block the blows and attacks of the enemy. It was used to provide a protective obstacle between the enemy and the soldier to absorb any attack. The *bulwark* refers to defensive fortifications surrounding the city to protect against any large-scale attack. For the soldier, his defenses had to be dependable. They would be useless if they collapsed as soon as the attack began.

For the one who dwells in the shelter of the Most High, God proves Himself to be faithful and reliable. No matter how powerful the attack, the reliability of God provides us with an indestructible and impenetrable defense. While we must take precautions in the face of threats, our ultimate security is not found in men's wisdom and actions, but in the sustaining promises of God. No matter what threat is confronting you today, if you are abiding in God, He stands between you and any danger, providing a protective shield that cannot be broken.

Day 2
The Faithfulness of God: The Hope of a Broken People

Lamentations 3:21–26

They are renewed every morning; great is Your faithfulness. Lamentations 3:23

Jeremiah was distraught and broken. Not only was he persecuted by the leaders of Judah, but he was brokenhearted that his people, the nation he loved, were thrown into bondage because of God's judgment upon them. For years Judah had continued their downward spiral into idolatry and rebellion against God. Time and time again, God had sent His prophets to warn them that they were descended into spiritual and moral chaos that it would end in their destruction. While there had been occasional glimpses of revival, they were short-lived; the people soon returned to the worship and religious practices of Baal. This religion incorporated temple prostitution and even child sacrifice. Much like today, the nation rejected the sanctity of marriage and life in their rebellious pursuit of foreign gods. Even when the northern tribes of Israel were cast into bondage because of their sins, the southern nation of Judah refused to heed the warning.

Consequently, God assigned the prophet Jeremiah the responsibility of proclaiming God's imminent and absolute judgment. The book of Lamentations was written in response to Judah's collapse and captivity in 586 BC when Babylon ravished the country and deported the people to become their slaves. So horrific was the nightmare of the siege that starvation and cannibalism became a daily reality for those trapped in the city of Jerusalem. Heartbroken by what was happening to the country and people he loved, Jeremiah, under the inspiration of the Holy

Spirit, penned his lament and grief over the downfall of Judah. In the heart of his lament, he felt the total weight of his affliction, which he describes as "my afflictions and my wandering, the wormwood and bitterness" (Lamentations 3:19).

Woven into the message of sorrow was also a prophetic message of hope. As Jeremiah pleaded for mercy and confessed the sins of his people, he contemplated the character of God. At the deepest and darkest time in Jeremiah's life, he recalled his God, and hope sprung to life again. Amid his sorrow, he remembered that God's loving-kindness never ceases, His compassion never fails, and that He remains ever faithful to His promises. Jeremiah again realized that the disciplining hand of God upon the nation did not mean that God had abandoned His covenant with Abraham. Even as God brought judgment upon the nation, He had not forgotten those who still faithfully sought Him and placed their trust in Him (vv. 25–26). God was always faithful to the righteous remnant, even as He brought judgment upon the nation. In verse 20, Jeremiah describes his soul as decaying within him; however, in verse 24, we find his soul-affirming words, "The LORD is my portion." For Jeremiah, God Himself was his greatest possession, and this is what gave him hope.

In times when it seems like everything around us is rapidly deteriorating, we have the hope and confidence that God will remain faithful to those trusting in Him. He still knows His people and faithfully watches over us. It is no wonder that Thomas Chisholm, whose continual poor health forced him out of ministry and caused him to struggle financially, found comfort in these words and would write one of the great hymns of the faith: "Great is thy faithfulness, O God my Father, there is no shadow of turning with Thee; Thou changest not, thy compassions they fail not, as thou hast been, thou forever will be. Great is thy faithfulness!" In our times of trouble, we have the same comfort: God's faithfulness is more than sufficient for any situation.

Day 3
The Faithfulness of God: The Call to Live Differently

Read Hebrews 10:1–25

Let us hold fast the confession of our hope without wavering, for He who promised is faithful. Hebrews 10:23

How should we live considering what Christ did on the cross? Each year we remember the death and resurrection of Christ when we celebrate Good Friday and Easter. This celebration raises two crucial questions. First, what is the significance of these events that make them worthy of our yearly celebration? Second, what difference do these events that happened two thousand years ago make for us today?

In Hebrews 10, the writer answers these two critical questions. In verses 1–18, the writer addresses the first question by contrasting the sacrifice of Christ with the sacrifices of the Old Testament. During the Old Testament period, the nation of Israel would conduct sacrifices every year on the Day of Atonement to obtain forgiveness for the people's sins. However, these offerings were only a temporary solution until the arrival of the total and final sacrifice. Therefore, Christ came to provide that final sacrifice. Because of His sacrifice on the cross, the justice of God was completely satisfied, and our sins are eternally forgiven. Therefore, no further sacrifice is needed. This was illustrated by Christ sitting down at God's right hand, thus signifying the end of the redemptive work (vv. 9–14).

We are now confronted with the second question. The writer addresses this question in verses 19–25, where he provides several practical implications. First, in verse 22, we find that we are to come into the presence of God confidently. This statement points us back to Hebrews 4:14–16, where we are encouraged to pray with confidence for God to provide mercy and grace in the hours of our desperate need.

We find in verse 23 that we are to remain steadfast in the confession of our faith. The phrase "without wavering" literally means not to bend or lean to one side or another and speaks of a firm resolution that is unshakable. We are reminded in these words of a mighty tree that is entirely untouched by the winds. No matter how strong the winds of adversity blow against it, it is so strong that it does not even sway. Likewise, no matter what we face in life, no matter how strong the attack upon our faith, we will not waver or doubt.

We are to maintain our fellowship with believers, recognizing that salvation is not just individual but a call to live in a community of mutual care and understanding. We do not attend church solely for our benefit and edification. Instead, we are to come to encourage and strengthen others.

In verse 23, we find the reason these events are still relevant today. The writer of Hebrews grounds these principles in the redemptive work of Christ and the faithfulness of God. Because God is faithful, we have assurance that the promises of Christ's redemption remain continually valid, even for us. Just as it was confirmed in the first century, we can also come before God with confidence in prayer. Because Christ's redemptive work still stands true, we are to remain steadfast in our faith.

Last, since God is always faithful, we can encourage others in their faith with the same hope that His faithfulness gives us. To understand the faithfulness of God is to radically change how we live. It means that both the promise and the way of living established in the Scriptures remain valid, for God's truth has not changed. When we are facing the winds of change and adversity, it is easy to waiver. However, the faithfulness of God gives us a rock upon which to ground our faith. This faith brings hope in the promises of God and a new way of living in light of His work.

Day 4
The Faithfulness of God: The Completion of Our Salvation

Read 1 Thessalonians 5:12–24

Faithful is He who calls you, and He also will bring it to pass. 1 Thessalonians 5:24

Sometimes the Christian life seems like a never-ending climb up an insurmountable mountain. We desire to grow in Christ and live in obedience to Him, but we fail continually and miserably. At times, as we face the struggles of life, the promises of God seem hollow and unattainable. Not that we abandon our faith—it is just that we are overwhelmed by the challenges we face. Paul was not any different. In 2 Corinthians 7:5, we read that "Even when we came into Macedonia our flesh had no rest, but we were afflicted on every side; conflicts without, fears within." What is striking in his confession is not that they faced many conflicts, for certainly Paul continually faced opposition from his persecutors. The surprise is his confession of the struggle against "fears within." This statement echoes what he had previously stated in 2 Corinthians 1:8: "We were burdened excessively, beyond our strength, so that we despaired even of life." In these words of Paul, we find that he was no different than the rest of us. The mighty Paul, who is seen as one of the great champions of the faith, was not above struggling with the same discouragement, depression, and anxiety that grips us when life seems to collapse around us. These are words we easily identify with as we face our own battles, both outward and internal. Like Paul, when we are going through difficulties in life, we can quickly feel overwhelmed as fear replaces faith in the uncertainty of the circumstances surrounding us.

So how did Paul rise above these things? What kept him going when he encountered these periods of his life? The answer lies in the passage before us today. In 1 Thessalonians 5:23, Paul prays that the God of peace would sanctify us entirely and that He would preserve us, spirit, soul, and body, so that we might obtain the full and final completion of God's redemptive purpose. In this verse, we see the full scope of our salvation. God did not just save us to give us eternal life. He redeemed us to completely transform our total being—spirits, emotions, and even our physical bodies. God desires that His holiness and purity would encompass our entire existence, allowing us to be wholly and radically transformed.

Being transformed to be like Christ seems impossible in our daily struggles. The Christian life often seems like the proverbial statement "one step forward and two steps back" as we struggle to find this transformational power for the daily realities of life. In our quest, Paul brings clarity and hope. In verse 24, he gives us the promise that God is faithful and that this transformation is not the work that we do in ourselves by our own resolve and strength; it is the work God himself achieves. Even as we struggle in our faith, God remains faithful, working as the unseen hand that brings about our complete transformation so that in the end, when we stand before Him, we will stand entirely sanctified. This hope is what enabled Paul to rise above the challenges he faced. His confidence was not in himself but in God, who remains faithful to continue to work in our lives. Even when God seems distant, we have assurance that He remains ever-present to guide us and strengthen us, and because He is faithful, He will not fail.

When you find fear and discouragement enveloping you, you can rest in a faithful God—a God who is continually working in your life to bring you to the point where you fully attain what He has promised you and desires for you. So today, as you are confronted with the challenges of life, remember that God is faithful, and these challenges are His instrument to achieve His purpose in you.

Day 5
The Faithfulness of God: The Forgiveness of Sin

Read 1 John 1:5–10

He is faithful and righteous to forgive us our sins. 1 John 1:9

How does sinful man stand in the presence of a holy God? This question is perhaps the most fundamental question of all religions and faiths. There is a universal acknowledgment that God is perfect and holy. Yet, the question that mystifies theologians and philosophers is the evil of humanity (not that we are as evil as we could be, but that we have all committed acts of sin and broken God's moral law). If God is holy, how does a holy God accept imperfect people marred by sin? It is this very question John seeks to answer. John begins with an affirmation of God's holiness by comparing His righteousness with the absolute brilliance of light. With God, there is no hint of darkness; there is no presence or touch of sin.

In contrast to the absolute holiness of God is our own sinfulness. John points out that the only way we can have fellowship with God is to be holy even as He is holy (which John compares to pure light; v. 7). But herein lies the great dilemma, for we are inherently sinful. To deny this is the ultimate self-deception and reveals that we have rejected the truth of God (v. 8). The flow of John's argument is this:

1. God is holy.
2. We can only have fellowship with God if we are holy.
3. We are all sinners and therefore unholy.

If he stopped there, we would be hopelessly lost in our sin. However, John provides hope and assurance that serve to answer the question perplexing all humanity. The way we stand before a holy God is by confessing our sin before Him. To confess is not merely to acknowledge our sin; it is to admit and recognize that we are indeed lawbreakers who are deserving of judgment. It is to realize that we deserve punishment and to accept that Christ paid the penalty for us (1 John 2:2).

Hope for our forgiveness is not grounded in our actions or our intrinsic goodness. Instead, it is in the faithfulness and righteousness (or justice) of God. The word translated as *righteous* refers to what is legally or ethically correct. In other words, because Christ paid the penalty of our sin, the justice of God has been satisfied, enabling us to be free from the judicial punishment of our acts of rebellion. But this brings us to His faithfulness. As we have seen throughout our study of God's faithfulness, this refers to God's faithfulness to His word and promises. Because God has given His promise to forgive us through the death of Christ, if we accept His forgiveness, we now have assurance that He will be faithful to fulfill this promise. We now have confidence before God, the certainty our sins are forgiven, no matter how great they might be. If our standing before God is based on our actions, then we are hopelessly lost, but because it is based on God's actions and promise, we have the absolute joy and confidence of our acceptance by God because He is always faithful to His promise. We are no longer under the guilt of our failures. We no longer need to fear God. We no longer need to try and earn God's favor. All that is required of us is to accept His forgiveness and rest joyfully within His assurance.

If you still feel the weight of guilt for your past, all you need to do is confess what you have done and ask God's forgiveness. His faithfulness provides the bedrock of assurance that He will cleanse you from all unrighteousness (1 John 1:9)

The Truthfulness of God

Yet those who wait for the LORD will gain new strength; they will mount up with wings like eagles.
Isaiah 40:31

How do we know what we know? The question may seem confusing and overly philosophical, but it touches upon one of the most fundamental of all problems: how do we determine what is true? In our modern age, many have turned to science as the final determination of truth. Scientific facts become the standard, and so we conform our beliefs to them. If the Bible, which presents a view of creation that is supernatural in origin, conflicts with the evolutionary process that science has proven (or at least proven in the minds of many), then we reinterpret the Bible. Thus, we turn to human reason and experience to determine truth. It is through our collective reasoning that we come to understand what is morally right and wrong. However, this has led us down the wrong path. In the last hundred years, our scientific advances, which have brought about great good, have also resulted in humanity killing more people than the previous nineteen hundred centuries combined.

The abandonment of biblical truth in favor of human reasoning is not new. From the very beginning of time, we have rejected God's revealed truth in favor of our rationale. What tempted

Adam and Eve in the garden, which had such allure that they would cast aside all that God had created for them, was the desire to be independent of God. What led us to rebel against God was our desire to determine our destiny. The two attributes of God that humanity rejected in the Garden of Eden were the sovereignty of God—that is, the right and authority to control all things, including our lives—and the truth of God, that God is the sole and final determiner of truth. We pick and choose which Bible verses we want to listen to and reject those we find uncomfortable. However, to say that the Bible contains error is to say that God communicated falsehood, and, in the end, it involves a denial of God's truthfulness.

In 2 Timothy 3:16–17, Paul affirms the truthfulness of Scripture by declaring that the Bible did not originate from the mind of man but from the mind of God. The Scriptures are true because they come from a God who is always true. When we affirm that truthfulness is intrinsic to the nature of God, we are affirming several vital facts about God. First, we confirm that God is true—that is, He is real and genuine. He is not fabricated by man or by our imagination. Jeremiah writes, "But the LORD is the true God. He is the living God and the everlasting King. At his wrath, the earthquakes, and the nations cannot endure His indignation. Thus, you shall say to them, 'The gods that did not make the heavens and the earth will perish from the earth and from under the heavens" (Jeremiah 10:10–11).

Second, God is truthful, in that everything he says is right and He is the ultimate source of all truth. "God is not a man, that He should lie, nor a son of man, that He should repent; has He said, and will He not do it? Or has He spoken, and will He not make it good" (Numbers 23:19). Therefore, because He is the source and standard of what is genuine and authentic, when God swore to fulfill His promise, He could swear by no greater measure of truth than Himself (Hebrews 6:13).

Third, because God cannot lie, we have hope and confidence. As the writer of Hebrews points out, "So that by two unchangeable things [His character and His word] in which it is impossible for God to lie, we who have taken refuge would have strong encouragement to take hold of the hope set before us. This hope we have as an anchor of the soul, a hope both sure and steadfast" (Hebrews 6:18–20). Because God is true and the source of all truth and cannot be associated with a lie, we know that His Word is always accurate and can be trusted. Christ points out that the truth of God's Word is so comprehensive that it encompasses every letter and every mark (Matthew 5:18).

The divine inspiration of Scripture leads us to three important facts regarding God's Word. First, the Bible is the foundation for all spiritual knowledge. Scientists refer to our DNA as the book of life, for our DNA governs who we are, our personality, and everything about us. If our DNA is the book of our physical lives, then the Bible is the book of our spiritual lives. The Scriptures provide instructions on how to live rightly before God. They confront us when we veer off course. They provide correction and training in righteousness. Second, because God is true, His Word is sufficient for our every need. Third, God has communicated His truth in such a way that we can understand. This does not mean that the Bible is simplistic, but that there is nothing hidden, nothing that is beyond our ability to understand.

The certainty of His Word provides you hope in your present struggles of life. God has provided His Word to give you guidance and direction. Because He is always truthful, you can rely upon His Word and trust that you will find what is true and correct in your obedience to His Word. So, when you are confused in life, go to the one place where you find truth and clarity—to God and His Word.

Day 1
The Truthfulness of God: God Is the True God

Read: Jeremiah 10:1–11

But the LORD *is the true God.* Jeremiah 10:10

We live in the age of imitations, knockoffs, and reproductions. Walk down the street of any tourist destination and you can find a host of vendors selling knockoffs that bear the name and appearance of their famous counterparts. However, look closely, and you will find that they are forgeries lacking the quality that marks the more expensive original.

We also live in the age of religious imitations. Today, in our post-modern worldview, all religions are seen to be equally valid. The mantra of the day is, "All religions lead to the same god, so it does not matter what you believe; it only matters that you believe." To say that there is only one God and one way to God is regarded as arrogant and exclusionary.

We are no different than past generations. Throughout the history of humanity, there has always been a plethora of religious views. It was no different in Jeremiah's time when the Israelites adopted other people's religious practices and beliefs. Consequently, the prophet Jeremiah arrived and, in satiric fashion, revealed the folly of the different religions and the genuineness of God. For Jeremiah, comparing the beliefs of the surrounding nations to the God of the Bible was like comparing a fifty-dollar Rolex imitation to the authentic Rolex that costs thousands of dollars. There just is no comparison. Compared to the God of the Bible, the other gods are nothing more than "scarecrows in a cucumber field" (Jeremiah 10:5).

To affirm that God is a God of truth is to uphold that He is the only true God. He is genuine, authentic, and not a fabrication of our imagination. All other gods are mere caricatures of the real thing. In the end, they are genuinely empty, for they cannot save and are merely the inventions of humanity to be a substitute for God. To say that all religions lead to the same God is like saying all watches are Rolexes. They may look similar, but in the end, they are vastly different. What distinguishes the God of the Bible and the gods of other religions is not the external forms but the nature and character of God. God alone is the living God and everlasting King who created the universe and will bring just and righteous judgment upon the earth (vv. 10–11). Thus, the question we must ask ourselves is not, "Do I believe in God?" but, "What God do I believe in?" The Lord is the one true God (v. 10).

When we face trials in our lives, they strip away the non-essentials and confront us with what is essential and what we believe. If we have not accepted the triune God revealed in the Bible, we follow a myth that will not lead us to God but away from Him. We follow that which makes promises but cannot deliver. All religions do not lead to God, for Christ himself stated, "I am the way, and the truth, and the life, no one comes to the Father but through Me" (John 14:6). There is only one God and only one way to God.

The first step in the journey is to acknowledge that the God of the Bible is the only true God. Because only He is God, you have a basis for certainty and hope. Therefore, you do not worship and believe in a dream or hope. Instead, your faith is riveted in an actual person who is the source of all truth. Therefore, you can have confidence in uncertain times.

Day 2
The Truthfulness of God: God's Word Is Truth

Read Psalm 119:145–152

And all Your commandments are truth. Psalm 119:151

Psalm 119 is the longest chapter in the Bible. Written in Hebrew as an acrostic, where each verse begins with a specific Hebrew letter, the chapter is a masterfully written celebration of the nature of God's Word and law. Heaping adjective upon adjective, the psalmist struggles to fully convey the Scriptures' depth, wonder, power, character, and impact. The psalmist desires to leave no stone unturned in his examination of the Word of God, and so he uses every possible term known to capture the breadth of Scripture. In just eight verses, he uses six different words that describe God's Word (statutes, testimonies, words, ordinances, law, commandments).

However, it is not just the scope of God's words that he desires to capture. He also aims to capture the whole range of impact that God's Word has upon the reader. There is no single human experience that the Bible does not help the reader to navigate (vv. 146–147). While the law of God provides moral clarity and guidance (see v. 119: 9), it also serves to revive us when life seems overwhelming and confusing. The word *revive* is derived from the Hebrew word for life (the term used for the infamous song in Fiddler on the Roof, *l'chaim*, or "to life"). It expresses a life that one enjoys to the fullest with health and prosperity. This life is grounded in drawing near to God (vv. 145–148) and in God drawing near to us (vv. 149–152).

In verse 151, we find the reason why the psalmist has such confidence in the life-giving power of the laws of God: "And all Your commandments are truth." The word *truth* refers to that which is dependable, reliable, and trustworthy—that is, not just true in the abstract sense of truth, but in the practical purpose as well. In other words, the law of God provides the correct answer for how we are to conduct ourselves in a way that honors God in a world that is fallen and rejects God.

When we speak of God being a God who is true, it not only means that He is the true God, but that He is a God of truth who cannot lie. Consequently, His Word is tested and proven (Proverbs 30:5). The Bible is not just a book written about truth or even a book that contains truth. The Bible is Truth (with a capital T) because it originates from God and is thus the standard of all truth. The words of Scripture cut through the muddled confusion of our lives and give us the correct answers. To reject the Bible is to embrace what is false, bringing death rather than life.

When we are confronted with confusion, the Bible provides us with the bedrock of truth that brings clarity. When faced with the perplexing questions of our society and our personal lives, the first and final source of guidance must come from Scripture. We read the newspaper to find out what is happening in our world. We need to read the Bible to learn how to live in our world. If you are confused about life and the struggles you are facing, turn to the pages of Scripture and ask God to bring you clarity, hope, and life from His Word. His words are life!

Day 3
The Truthfulness of God: Discovering the Will of God

Read John 17:13–26

Sanctify them in the truth; Your word is truth. John
17:17

One of the most significant challenges we face in dealing with adversity is struggling to find answers. When we face struggles, we often find our self-reliance being stripped away as we strive to make sense of the events pressing upon us. We wrestle to know what God is doing, why He allows these events to happen, and what His purpose is. We struggle to know His will when we do not even know what the next day will hold. How can we know God's will when we don't have any answers in life?

In John 17:13–26, Christ prays for His followers to discover insight into God's will, especially when questions are overwhelming and answers are elusive. The heart of Christ's prayer, and His defining purpose for all His disciples, is found in verse 17: that God would "sanctify them in the truth; Your word is truth." This purpose of sanctification stands at the heart of God's redemptive plan. While justification is the act of God in which He declares us judicially free from the guilt of sin, sanctification is the work of God in which He progressively conforms us to the image of Christ. For the New Testament writers, this is the foundation upon which the whole Christian life, and God's activity within that life, are built. In this process, we are changed from conforming to the world to adopting the character of Christ. It is the life of faith practiced daily (see Romans 12:1–2; Galatians 2:20; 2 Corinthians 5:17).

In Christ's prayer, He points the way to how this is achieved. It is accomplished through the knowledge and application of the truth of God's Word. God is a God of truth who requires us to conform to His standard. This standard is revealed in His Word. However, the truth of God does not consist of static, impersonal facts to which we intellectually give our agreement. It is not like a scientist who affirms specific facts governing creation's laws but goes home unchanged by His discovery. Instead, the truth of God is dynamic, living, and life-changing. To know the truth of God is to be transformed by His truth. Conforming to Christ only happens when His Word changes us. For this reason, the study of Scripture is foundational to being a disciple and follower of Christ. Any attempt to follow Christ apart from the truth of God's Word will ultimately end in the very opposite—conformity to the world.

As we are going through the struggles of life, we cannot always answer the immediate question of *why*, nor are we able to answer questions of what we ought to do. Nevertheless, we can always know the answer to the question regarding God's intended purpose and outcome. His purpose in all things is to conform us to His image by using the uncertainty of our experiences to remind us to seek the truth of His Word continually.

The most crucial step when going through tribulation is not finding the correct answers, but asking the right questions. The most important question, the one question that should send you back to the Bible, is, "How can I reveal Christ through my life and in this present crisis?" That is the question you need to ask yourself today.

Day 4
The Truthfulness of God: The God Who Guides Us in the Truth

Read John 16:5–15

But when He, the Spirit of truth, comes, He will guide you into all the truth. John 16:13

For three years, the disciples enjoyed instruction from Christ daily. For three years, Christ guided them with His infinitely wise counsel, giving insight from the Scriptures to help them navigate the challenges they faced. Every time they were confused or perplexed, they could turn to Christ, and He would bring clarity and perspective. But then Christ announced the unthinkable. As they gathered to celebrate the Passover, Christ informed them that He would be betrayed and would be leaving them. Fear, anxiety, and confusion swept through their minds as they faced the prospect of going forward without the guidance of the one whom they had devoted their lives to follow.

The fear and confusion that gripped their minds that evening were no different than the chaos that plagues our thoughts when life becomes unpredictable and unmanageable. In the end, we are left with the conclusion that truth is elusive and unknowable. With all the different conflicting views being propagated, how can we know if anything is true? We wonder, like the disciples did that night, are we left to blindly navigate a life where there is no objective truth, only the truth that we can determine ourselves? In a world of conflicting narratives, many have concluded that truth is relative. While we affirm that God is a God of truth, how can we, as fallen individuals, ever be able to determine what is right?

Even as we struggle (along with the disciples) to understand what Christ was saying, Christ gives us a promise: that we are not abandoned to figure out our own ways in life. Instead, we are given another guide who is present by our sides each step of the way. He will direct us in the truth—not that He will simply help us understand what to do, but He will guide us in how to live within the truth of God. But this brings us to the critical question: how do we discern the leading of the Holy Spirit from the plethora of voices we hear in our society today? The answer lies in the study of the Bible. The Holy Spirit guides us in our understanding of Christ, His redemptive work, and how we are to live in response to Christ as we read His Word.

Herein lies our greatest danger. In our quest for truth, instead of searching Scriptures, we turn to our own reasoning. Proverbs warn us of the risk of relying upon our own wisdom to guide us. Proverbs 14:12 states, "There is a way which seems right to a man, but its end is the way of death." To trust in our thoughts is ultimately self-deceptive. Jeremiah 17:9 states, "The heart is more deceitful than all else and is desperately sick; who can understand it?" If this is the case, then what hope do we have? The answer brings us back to the work of the Holy Spirit, the study of Scripture, and the humble acknowledgement of our need for guidance. In Psalm 25:4–5, we find the prayer that we desperately need to pray daily:

"Make me know Your ways, O LORD; teach me Your paths. Lead me in your truth and teach me, for you are the God of my salvation, for you, I wait all day." When this becomes our prayer, and the Scriptures become the object of our search, we have the assurance that the Holy Spirit will guide us in the truth.

Day 5
The Truthfulness of God: Finding Freedom in His Truth

Read John 8:31–39

You will know the truth, and the truth will make you free. John 8:32

What does it mean to be free? As we see the world around us descend into chaos, we struggle to understand freedom. For many, freedom is the right to live as we please, pursuing our impulses and passions without any restraint or consequence. For others, freedom is merely a façade concealing racial and economic disparities that bring freedom to some and bondage to others. While these continue to be important discussions in our society, Christ points us to a more profound freedom, one that is the foundation for life itself. When Christ offered them freedom, the Jews were perplexed. Why was Jesus talking about the necessity of liberty when they were not enslaved to anyone? For them, freedom was ethnic, not being under the domination of Gentiles. Yet they missed the whole point Christ was making, for there is a more profound and more powerful bondage we face than being enslaved to another. That deeper bondage is found in our enslavement to sin. In John 8:34, Christ points out that we become enslaved to sin when we give in to its temptation. Sin is always a terrible and demanding taskmaster. While sin gives us the allure of freedom, in the end, it dominates and leads us down a road of personal and spiritual destruction. In our culture today, we fail to realize that we are selling ourselves to enslavement in our quest for individual freedom. The more we demand the right to have the freedom of our own moral choices, the more enslaved we become to those choices.

Christ gives us hope, and that hope is found in the truth of God. As we have seen in this study, God is the true God, He is the one who determines truth, and He has communicated this to us in His Scriptures so that we might know and live by His Word. This truth is not restrictive; instead, it brings freedom in the truest sense of the word. True freedom is not found in the choice to do as we please; rather, it is the liberty to do as God pleases; it is the freedom to do what is right. This liberation is only found in being a disciple of Christ. When we become His disciples, He gives us the greatest freedom of all—the emancipation from the tyranny of our sinful passions and choices. If we want true freedom that liberates the soul, it does not come by giving license to our desires; it comes by surrendering to Christ and His Word. This is the paradox of faith. The more we relinquish ourselves to Christ, the more liberated we become; the more we give freedom to our desires, the more enslaved we become by them. Charles Wesley's hymn "And Can It Be" captures this perfectly: "Long my imprisoned spirit lay fast bound in sin and nature's night; Thine eye diffused a quick'ning ray, I woke, the dungeon flamed with light; My chains fell off, my heart was free; I rose, went forth, and followed Thee." To obtain true freedom today, surrender to Christ and seek His truth, and He will give you ultimate freedom.

The Fatherhood of God

Then I said, "How I would set you among My sons and give you a pleasant land, the most beautiful inheritance of the nations!" And I said, "You shall call me My Father and not turn from following Me."
Jeremiah 3:19

One of the most staggering teachings of the New Testament, a radical shift from the Old Testament, was the teaching that we now relate to God as our Father. In the Old Testament, there are only fifteen times when God is specifically referred to as the Father of the nation of Israel or individuals. In the Old Testament, the focus was more on God's covenant-keeping nature, the one who made a promise to His people and was always faithful to that promise.

In the New Testament, the focus changed with the teaching of Christ. When Christ came, He was the Son of God, and so His favorite term for addressing God was to refer to Him as his Father (Christ refers to God as His Heavenly Father one hundred sixty-five times in the Gospels). By referring to God as Father, He changed the focus from God being the covenant God to the intimate relationship existing between the Father and the Son. In light of our identification with Christ and our union with Him, this also changed the focus of our relationship with God. Paul refers to God as our Father forty times in his writings. He highlights this new focus in Romans 8:14–15 when he affirms that we are no longer slaves to sin, but now we are sons of God. Because of this new standing before God, we can cry out to him as "Abba, Father." The word *Abba* conveys a sense of intimacy and familiarity with God. It changes our relationship and approach to God from the formal association of a subject coming before a king to the informal, intimate relationship of a child running to the arms of his loving father. This new title, "Abba," is significant because it was the term Jesus used when praying to the Father. This brings us a new perspective of our relationship with God. Before Christ, God's relationship with the people of Israel was grounded in the Old Testament covenant and the sacrificial system. However, because we are united with Christ, we are now fellow heirs with Christ, which brings a new relationship with the Father. We have a child's boldness before the Father rather than the fear and apprehension of a subject before a king. We are now His children, and as His children, He pours out His love and cares for us.

We now have a new hope. Perhaps the most surprising and perplexing implication of this new relationship with God is that we are now co-heirs with Christ. As an heir, Christ possesses all that the Father has, including all the blessings and joys of sharing in the life of the Father. He has an eternal relationship, one grounded in love, fellowship, and the pleasure of a mutual relationship, an outgrowth of the unity within the triune Godhead. As co-heirs with Christ, we are now invited to share in this relationship. To be a co-heir with Christ means that we now have the same status and relationship that Christ has with the Father. All that Christ claims as His own is now given freely to us. This promise gives us hope that transports us beyond the present struggles we face. We have in store for us an inheritance that is unparalleled, eternal, and undiminishing (1 Peter 1:4). This inheritance is not based upon our merits but upon God's grace and compassion for us (Colossians 1:12).

The hope of our inheritance is what enables us to rise above the sufferings we have at present (Romans 8:18). We suffer in the present because we still live in a world dominated and marred by sin. The world and universe are slowly decaying and dying as sin brings its destructive consequence. As a result, "We groan within ourselves, waiting eagerly for our adoption as sons, the redemption of our body" (Romans 8:23). However, the present suffering only serves to highlight further the hope that we have in store. God did not just save us from the punishment of hell; He saved us to an eternal inheritance that is now reserved for us. Therefore, amid our adversity, we persevere with hope because we already have the promise of our inheritance.

Day 1
The Fatherhood of God: God's Proof of His Love

Read 1 John 3:1–16

See how great a love the Father has bestowed on us . . . that He laid down His life for us. 1 John 3:1,16

In the song "The Wreck of the Edmond Fitzgerald," about a ship that was lost in a massive storm on Lake Superior, the songwriter, Gordon Lightfoot, asks the question, "Does anyone know where the love of God goes when the waves turn the minutes to hours?" This question haunts our minds during times of prolonged and intense struggles. Yet, perhaps the most challenging problem confronting our faith is the question, "How can a loving God allow us to face such difficulties in life?" The question is perplexing, and the answer is elusive. While not answering the question directly, John does give us the foundation for regaining the proper perspective. In 1 John 3:1, John affirms the lavish love God poured out on us when He gave us the privilege of becoming His children. The emphasis of this declaration is that this event is a firm, unchanging, completed act. We are now the permanent objects of His familiar love.

Furthermore, He is the one who initiated this new relationship rather than it being a result of our efforts or works (see also John 1:12–13). When God affirmed that He is our Father and legally adopted us as His children (Galatians 4:4–5), we entered into a completely new relationship with God. He no longer relates to us as the Creator interacts with His creation. Instead, He now associates with us as a loving Father relates to His children.

John now addresses another question: what is the proof that this love is genuine? In times when our circumstances seem to contradict His watchful care, and heaven seems silent, what is the anchor upon which we can secure our faith? The answer is found in verse 16. The proof of His love is located at the cross when Christ died for us. In 1 John 4:9–10, John further provides the certainty of His love when he states, "By this, the love of God was manifested in us, that God has sent His only begotten Son into the world so that we might live through Him. In this is love, not that we loved God, but that He loved us and sent His Son to be the propitiation [i.e., the substitutionary sacrifice] for our sins." In other words, the cross was the final and absolute proof of His love. If God's love moved Him to meet our most profound need—the need for salvation—then His love will motivate Him to meet our daily needs. No matter how silent heaven may seem, no matter how distant God may appear to us in our trials of life, we have assurance that He is ever-present, ever engaged, ever a loving and doting Father. He hovers over us to provide His care and protection.

In the wakeful hours of the night, when sleep is fleeting as our minds distress over the events that press upon us, we find rest by looking at the cross. While we still do not fully realize all that God has in store for us (v. 2), we have the confidence and assurance that we will be wholly transformed to share in His character and live eternally as His children in His presence. This is our hope and what gives us perspective in the present (v. 3). When you become overwhelmed with the worries of the day, just remember who your Father is and what He has promised you. Trust Him to give you strength each day so that nothing can harm you in the night.

Day 2
The Fatherhood of God: The Father Who Cares for Us

Read Matthew 7:7–11

How much more will your Father who is in heaven give what is good to those who ask him! Matthew 7:11

When I was a child, there was nothing better than a half sandwich left in a metal lunchbox sitting in the sun all day. When my dad came in from working in the fields all day, we would rush to his lunchbox to see if there was anything left, for his sandwiches were regarded by us as one of the exquisite delicacies of modern cooking. Surprisingly, there was often something left that we would then enjoy with rapturous delight. It was not until I was much older and reflecting on those discoveries that I realized it was not because mom always gave him more in his lunch than he could eat. The reason there was often some tasty morsel left was because my dad knew we would be looking. It was a father thinking of how a little leftover lunch brought joy to his children. Then, when I had children of my own, I too discovered the joy of giving to my children.

In Matthew, we find Christ comparing our heavenly Father to our earthly Father. As a father, it is our delight to give our children what they need for daily life *and* to give them those things that bring them joy. As a father, there are many times when we make small sacrifices (sometimes even immense sacrifices) just to bring delight to our children. In this context, Christ highlights the necessities of the children. Any father would respond to his child's basic needs—such as the need for daily food—by providing for them. Furthermore, it would be unthinkable that the father would give his children something harmful in the face of their basic needs.

Christ then draws the application. If a human father, who is marred by sin, desires to give his children good gifts, how much more does our heavenly Father, driven by infinite love for us, desire to give us beyond what we need? As our heavenly Father, God delights in giving us those things that bring us joy. Consequently, in verse 7, we are given the invitation to ask. But this invitation is not a blank check that God will do whatever we ask for in our selfish, pleasure-driven passions. The words *ask*, *seek*, and *knock* are rich in meaning as they progress in focusing upon our relationship with Him. First, the word *ask* focuses on simple prayer and requests. God invites us into an open and honest dialogue where we share with Him our needs and desires. Second, the word *seek* takes this prayer a step further. To seek is to go on a spiritual quest of seeking God and His kingdom (Matthew 6:33). It is not just to pursue what we want; it is to seek God Himself. Last, the word *knock* suggests that one is knocking on the door of God's residence to gain entrance into His presence.

God is wise enough (as are our earthly fathers) to know that giving us what we want will often harm us. So instead, as a loving Father, God desires to provide us with the greatest gift of all: the gift of Himself and a personal relationship with Him. In times of uncertainty and difficulty, it is easy to sacrifice the greater (our relationship with God) in search of the lesser (freedom from adversity). However, God does much more, for in our pain, He promises His presence, comfort, guidance, and help—all we have to do is ask! So, instead of praying for what we want (material prosperity and a trouble-free life), ask God to give you Himself. That is a prayer that He delights in answering.

Day 3
The Fatherhood of God: The Personal Knowledge of the Loving Father

Read Matthew 10:24–32

The very hairs of your head are all numbered. So do not fear. Matthew 10:30

The disciples must have felt apprehensive. In Matthew 10, we find Jesus sending the disciples by pairs on their first missionary venture. They were to go throughout the nation of Israel, proclaiming the arrival of the kingdom of heaven and calling people to repentance. His expressive words in verses 16–23, that they were going as sheep among wolves (hardly a picture one wants to envision as they start a new ministry), would have elicited fear in the bravest of them. Rather than giving them promises of success, Christ instead promised them that they would be beaten, hated, and arrested. Considering such a promise, it would have been seriously tempting to go back to fishing.

Recognizing their fear, Christ reminded them of His divine authority. Christ commissioned them to proclaim His message; consequently, they were not to be afraid to preach the kingdom of God openly. Furthermore, they were comforted by the fact that the Father had an intimate knowledge of their lives. Our heavenly Father is not some indifferent deity who merely gives an occasional glance in our direction to see what is going on. God is wholly engaged in the affairs of His world. Therefore, even the sparrows are of value to God.

How much more valuable are His followers? To emphasize both the value God places upon us and the knowledge He has of every detail of our lives, He points to the most insignificant aspect of our lives—the number of hairs on our heads. Our Father's interest in our lives delves into the most minor and trivial details. Because he is that attentive, we should not be afraid.

This perspective changes our view of suffering. As a loving father is ever watchful over his children, so our heavenly Father is watching over us. We are so valuable to Him that He continually remains alert to every circumstance we face. Psalm 56:8 states, "You have taken account of my wanderings; Put my tears in Your bottle. Are they not in Your book?" God is never indifferent, never forgetful, never distracted from His watchful care. This is why we do not need to fear, for God is sovereignly overseeing every facet, circumstance, and situation in our lives, and He is orchestrating all things to achieve His purpose in our lives. Therefore, we are not to allow present adversity to cloud our eternal perspective. Today, as you face the challenges of life, remember that God, as your attentive Father, pays close attention to every circumstance you are facing. If God cares for the sparrows and what happens to them, how much more does He care for you, and what is happening in your life today!

Day 4
The Fatherhood of God: The Foundation of Unity

Ephesians 4:1–6

One God and Father of all who is over all and through all and in all. Ephesians 4:6

As we look about us, we see our society descending into the abyss of conflict and division. At every turn, there seems to be a fracture separating people from one another. Our country is divided along political lines, cultural expressions, moral standards, and racial tensions. The tragedy is that amid these divisions, people have developed an us-versus-them mindset. If you are not for us, then you are against us. How can we find a basis of unity when there is no longer any dialogue or mutual respect?

While this is not surprising in the world, for we live in a world where sin has distorted our thinking and attitudes, the tragedy is that it can creep into the church. Instead of being shaped by a biblical worldview, we are shaped and influenced by our culture, politics, and society. When these become the focus, we quickly become divided within the church. In all this, we miss the most crucial question, and that is, "In an age of division and conflict, how can we find a basis of unity?"

This is the question that Paul is dealing with in Ephesians 4. Paul was no stranger to conflict. In his dealings with the various churches, he had dealt with congregations divided over many different issues. Paul understood that the threat of division could undermine the effectiveness of the church. As a result, he appeals to the church at Ephesus "to preserve the unity of the Spirit in the bond of peace" (Ephesians 4:3). However, Paul is not promoting a unity that comes at the cost of the gospel's truths; instead, it is grounded in the gospel message and sound doctrine (v. 5). But the climax of his call for unity is reached in verse 6: we find our harmony in the truth that there is one God and one Father of all. Furthermore, God is not only the Father of the Christians but also of all creation (see also vv. 14–15). God is the one who created all things and is the one through whom all things exist, and He stands transcendent over all things. It is the recognition that He rules over all creation and governs the universe to fulfill His purpose that unites us.

In the divided and conflicted world, the church displays God's rule by demonstrating unity. When we become separated by our differences, we are to remember what unites us. The world is divided and remains so because it has no foundation to connect people. Because we have God as our Father, we have a more profound truth to unite us together despite our differences. Our differences pale compared to the unity we have in God as our heavenly Father. The challenge we face in our age of diverse perspectives is to focus on God as our Father and remember our family heritage. When we allow our different opinions to divide us, we have lost sight of God's position in our lives. When our focus is upon God and the centrality of the gospel, then our differences become insignificant. The foundation for finding common ground upon which to build unity begins with accepting God's preeminent position in the universe and the foundation of his gospel. When confronting the challenges of our differences, remember that our common faith in Christ is more meaningful. This unity, centered on the gospel of Christ and the Fatherhood of God, is what we must display to a divided world.

Day 5
The Fatherhood of God: The Father Who Loves Us Enough to Discipline Us

Read Hebrews 12:1–11

He disciplines us for our good, so that we may share His holiness. Hebrews 12:10

There are many reasons why we experience painful events in our lives. First, we suffer because we live in a fallen world where sickness, death, and tragedy are part of our existence. Second, we experience struggles at times because of our identification with Christ (see the lives of Job and Paul). Finally, we face adversity because it is part of God's orchestrating of His plan (see the life of Joseph). Yet, we often overlook that one of the reasons we suffer is God's loving discipline.

When a couple has a child, it does not take long to realize that they need loving discipline. However, discipline is never enjoyable, either for the child or the parent. For the child, discipline seems harsh and unjust (few children ever say thank you after chastisement). It is painful as a parent to cause our children, whom we love and would readily sacrifice our lives to protect, to suffer. Yet, we realize that in order to be genuinely loving, we must be willing to discipline. One of the most unloving things we can do is give our children free rein without any guidance or correction. It is a recipe for disaster. A genuinely loving parent understands that a child is a sinner by nature and needs correction in order to learn the discipline of controlling their sinful impulses. Love is not blind to sin.

The writer of Hebrews compares the loving relationship between a parent and a child with our relationship with God. First, we need to recognize that God's love is purposeful. While God accepts us despite our failures and sins, He does not accept or ignore our sins. God's grace should never be mistaken for blind acceptance of evil. Instead, God saves us to transform us into His image, which is grounded in His holiness. This is what brings us to the Fatherhood of God. In Hebrews 12:1–2, the writer challenges us to set aside the sin entangling us and pursue the person of Christ, seeking to develop His character within us. Yet, how do we get from point A (a life trapped in sin) to point B (a life lived in fellowship with Christ and revealing His character)? The answer lies in the loving discipline of our heavenly Father. He recognizes that we cannot make this transition independently; we need His loving correction.

Consequently, God uses the struggles and trials we face to bring about this change. When God allows hardships, it is not because He is angry, indifferent, or even unloving. It is the very opposite. First, it is proof that we are His children (v. 7). Second, it reveals that He loves us enough to bring His disciplining hand so that we might attain the greatest gift of all, the invitation to share His holiness (v. 10). Not that our suffering brings us joy, but the travail we face achieves within us that which, in the end, brings the ultimate joy: the attainment of righteousness (v. 11).

In times of difficulty, take hope. Adversity does not mean that God has abandoned you or forgotten you; instead, it is proof of the very opposite. When you face trials, remember that God, like any loving Father, allows you to face problems and difficulties to mold and shape you to become like Him. As you face the challenges you encounter, ask God to give you insight into what He is doing in your life and how, through this experience, you can learn to trust Him more.

The Sovereignty of God

Who enclosed the sea with doors when . . . I said,
"Thus far you shall come, but no farther; and here
shall your proud waves stop"?
Job 38:8–11

U nderstanding and accepting the sovereignty of God has always been a challenge for people. Yet, it is the one attribute that can bring comfort in trials and cause us to question God. In times of uncertainty, we find comfort in the fact that God is in control of all the events of our lives. However, when we start talking about the loss of our freedom, we chafe at the idea that He is in control. We want a God who controls the universe, but not our own lives. We want the freedom to do as we please but the comfort that God is in control. Thus, we face the paradox of faith.

To understand the sovereignty of God, we must first understand what it is not. God's sovereign control is not fatalism. Fatalism is the idea that God predetermines every action and that His determination is arbitrary and capricious. However, God's control of the universe is never random or impulsive; His love governs it with purpose and design. While He gives us freedom of choice, He never relinquishes His complete control in guiding our lives to fulfill His purpose.

To affirm God's sovereignty is to confirm that God is in complete control of all things, at all times, and in all events. While He may choose to allow events to happen according to the natural laws He has established, He remains in control of the whole universe. God is infinite in all His attributes. Thus, to say that God is not in absolute control over all things places a limit upon His sovereignty. If we have any freedom of choice, it is because God allows us to have that choice, not because He lacks the authority to be in control. This has several important implications for our view of life and the world.

First, His sovereign control of humanity's affairs begins with His authority over nations and leaders. While God uses people's actions (by voting or appointment), all leaders are put in position by God. He determines who is in power and the extent of their control (Acts 17:26). Furthermore, He guides and directs leaders to accomplish His purpose (Proverbs 21:1). For the Christian, we no longer need to live in fear of the outcomes of elections; we have assurance that no matter what direction the political winds may blow, God is the one who ultimately determines the outcome.

Second, God is in control over the events that happen in our lives. In 1 Samuel 2:6–8, we read, "The Lord kills and makes alive, He brings down to Sheol and raises up. The Lord makes poor and rich; He brings lows; He also exalts. He raises the poor from the dust, He lifts the needy from the ash heap to make them sit with nobles and inherit a seat of honor; for the pillars of the earth are the Lord's, and He sets the world on them." From our perspective, life seems arbitrary, governed and guided by random events that unknowingly set our lives on a certain path. However, in God's sovereignty, we find comfort in knowing that our lives are not arbitrary, and that the rule of our lives are not determined by chance. Instead, it is guided by a sovereign God moving and directing our lives through the events that occur.

Third, God is sovereign in His redemptive plan. In Ephesians 1:3–6, Paul informs us that God's sovereign work in our salvation began even before the creation of the world. This teaching has resulted in countless debates by theologians regarding the relationship between God's sovereignty and man's freedom of will. Yet, in all the discussion, we miss the most crucial point that Paul is making: that God has a plan for our lives, and that that plan has a purpose—to integrate us into His family. He has chosen us to be His sons and daughters. God's plan becomes the basis of our hope. Either God is in control and sovereign over the events that happen in our lives, or the circumstances and events themselves control us. If God is in control, we have the certainty that our lives have purpose and design, and that everything that happens is overseen by a loving God who is moving us in the direction that is best. If our lives are controlled by chance, we have no certainty that the outcome will be good, for life is governed by chance rather than design. While we may not always understand God's purpose—and while we may not always see meaning in life's events—we have assurance that there is nothing arbitrary about it. When we go through trials and adversity, we know that God is still in control, guiding those events to move us in the best direction.

Day 1
The Sovereignty of God: The Victory Song of the Ages

Read Revelation 19:1–6

Hallelujah! For the Lord our God, the Almighty, reigns. Revelation 19:1

When we want to capture the joy of a celebration, there is something inherent within us that drives us to do so with a song. Think of the songs at a wedding, a holiday, or a special event. What would Christmas be without Christmas carols, or a Fourth of July celebration without the "Star-Spangled Banner" and "God Bless America"? What would graduation be without "Pomp and Circumstance"? It has been said that music is the language of the soul. However, what song will be sung at the end of the age when Christ comes in all His glory to establish His kingdom?

In Revelation 19:1–6, we stand at the threshold of the return of Christ. The judgment of God has been fully poured out, and now the multitudes in heaven, who have long waited for this event, join together in singing a four-stanza anthem of praise for Christ. The first stanza (vv. 1–2) celebrates the righteousness of God as He brings both final salvation for His people and judgment upon sin. The second stanza (v. 3) celebrates the final, complete, and eternal judgment poured out upon the city of Babylon, which stands in opposition to God. The third stanza (v. 4), sung by the twenty-four elders and four living beings, is a simple song of praise. Finally, the melodic anthem reaches its crescendo in the fourth stanza (v. 6) when all the multitudes sing forth with such a cacophony that it is compared to earthshaking peals of thunder. This final song, one serving to provide the climax of praise to God, is the celebration of the sovereign reign of God.

As we have seen, but continually need to be reminded of, when we speak of the sovereign reign of God, we are referring to the reality that God is always in control, over all things and over all events within all the universe. Revelation 19:1, coming at the end of time, serves to remind us that nothing is arbitrary or governed by chance, but rather that all of history is governed by a sovereign God who moves all things toward His predetermined conclusion. To affirm His sovereignty is to acknowledge what is recognized in this anthem: that God is the absolute and highest ruler in the universe who is unhindered in the exercise of His reign. He is not just an indifferent ruler who governs with arbitrary laws and misguided plans. Rather, He is a God who determines and accomplishes His will without restraint and with purpose and design.

God's unalterable will becomes our comfort and source of encouragement. No matter what happens in our lives and in our world, God remains enthroned in heaven, and He is sovereignly in control of our lives. So often, in the face of struggles, we feel powerless. It appears that chance and circumstances dictate the direction of our lives. Yet, this song of His sovereignty brings a different perspective. It serves to remind us that God is directing all of the events in the world and in our lives to move us to a climactic conclusion when He establishes His physical reign on the earth. This is our comfort in a broken world. Our lives are not a series of random events where chance and circumstance dictate the outcomes. Our lives are under the sovereign control of God, who guides and directs us through the exercise of His love and purpose. He has a plan and a goal for history and our individual lives, so in turn we can rejoice and rest in Him. We, too, will join with the multitudes at the end of the age celebrating His righteous sovereignty. Today, when it seems your life is out of control, remember who is in control and ask Him to guide you in His plan and purpose.

Day 2
The Sovereignty of God: The Hope of Our Salvation

Read Ephesians 1:1–12

> *He chose us in Him before the foundation of the world, that we would be holy and blameless before him.* Ephesians 1:4

Perhaps the most perplexing doctrine in Scripture is the sovereign election of God. Theologians have debated the doctrine for centuries as they try to understand the relationship between God's sovereignty and humanity's freedom of choice. They continue to argue the question, "Did we choose God because He first chose us, or did God choose us because we chose Him? At the center of the debate regarding the sovereignty of God stands Ephesians 1:1–12. While the debate has raged for generations and will undoubtedly continue until the Lord returns, the tragedy is that some of the greatest truths of Scripture have been overlooked amid the discussion. Rather than it being a source of conflict, when we read this passage carefully it becomes foundational for our hope and salvation in Christ.

While the debate continues to rage regarding the meaning and timing of the words "chose" and "predestined," what we dare not miss is the purpose and goal of our salvation as expressed in these verses. The benefits of our salvation highlighted in these verses are beyond comprehension. We have been blessed with every spiritual blessing in the heavenly places (v. 3). We are chosen to become holy and blameless (v. 4). Because of God's love for us, we are adopted to be His children (v. 5). We are the recipients of His grace, which He freely bestows upon us (v. 6). We are redeemed from the slavery of sin (v. 7) and forgiven of all our sins (v. 7). He has lavishly poured out His grace upon us (vv. 7–8). We have insight into His divine will and purpose (v. 9). God has granted us an inheritance (v. 11). Christ has provided His hope to us (v. 12). The list goes on. It goes beyond our ability to truly comprehend the full depth of what He has given us and promised us in our salvation.

The basis of these promises is not grounded in our ability and actions, but in the sovereign work of God. When Paul states that God chose us (v. 4) and predestined us (vv. 5, 11), He provides the foundation of our confidence. The word "predestined" means to determine something ahead of time or before it occurs. Before God spoke the world into existence (v. 4), He already has us in His mind's eye and already determined His purpose for us. In a world seemingly driven by chaos and circumstance, God does not leave our salvation to chance. Instead, His sovereignty moves us to the realization of His purpose for our lives. Rather than seeing His sovereignty as a threat to our freedom, it is the foundation of our confidence and joy. Because He has already determined the outcome, we have *certainty*, no matter how circumstances may seem to undermine our hope for the future. It serves to remind us that with God, there is no coincidence, life is not determined by luck, and our salvation is not just the fantasy of an idealist. To surrender to Christ and His plan is not to give up our freedom and dreams; it is how we fully realize them.

As we are going through the uncertainty of the day, it is easy to become fearful because we do not know what will happen tomorrow. Nevertheless, when we rest in God's sovereign purpose, we already know the outcome, and this gives us hope for the present—a hope that is not a pipedream, but a deep conviction that God has already determined the conclusion.

Day 3
The Sovereignty of God: The One Who Controls the Nations

Read Daniel 2

It is He who changes the times and epochs; He removes kings and establishes kings. Daniel 2:21

Daniel 2 remains one of the most remarkable prophetic chapters in the Bible. Nebuchadnezzar woke from his sleep deeply troubled by a dream he could not remember. Not being able to recall the dream, Nebuchadnezzar summoned all his royal magicians, astrologers, and wise men and commanded them not just to tell him the meaning of the dream but also to reveal the vision itself. When they pointed out the task's impossibility, he became furious and decreed to have them all torn limb from limb. Although Daniel and his three friends were not present when the demand was made, they were likewise included in the death sentence since they were among of the king's wise men.

In a remarkable feat, revealing the genuineness of the God of Israel, God revealed to Daniel both the dream and the interpretation. The detail with which Daniel revealed the future events encompassing the Ancient Near East has amazed biblical scholars and confounded secular historians who reject the notion of prophetic revelation. In the interpretation, Daniel outlined with fantastic accuracy the history of nations from the time of the Babylonians to the establishment of the Roman Empire, culminating in the yet future establishment of the messianic King, which yet remains in the prophetic future of God's redemptive plan. Thus, the unfolding of history would encompass four great kingdoms beginning with the Babylonians (vv. 36–38). They would reign until 539 BC, when the alliance of the Medes and the Persians, led by Cyrus the Great, would defeat them (v. 39a). After that, the Medo-Persian Empire would dominate the region until 331 BC A third nation would then arise (v. 39b), rapidly conquering the civilized world of the day. This prophecy was fulfilled when Alexander the Great swept through the whole region and brought the Ancient Near East under the control of the Greeks from 331 BC until 146 BC. However, their reign would end when the Roman Empire defeated them at the Battle of Carthage (vv. 40–43)—thus, the fourth kingdom predicted by Daniel. The messianic King will crush this final kingdom and will establish an eternal kingdom still in the prophetic future (vv. 44–45).

This remarkable prophecy was not based upon Daniel's blind luck to predict the political scene of the future. Nor was it written by some later redactor who would merely record the Ancient Near East's history and attribute it to Daniel. Instead, the prophetic history was orchestrated and revealed by a God who is sovereign over the affairs of nations. He determines the history of countries and the establishment of political leaders (v. 21). This provides us confidence and hope in an age of political uncertainty and division. We see the conflicts in our nation and our politicians' divisions, reflected in different public policies and different worldviews. We know the turmoil caused by political movements that desire to fundamentally dismantle and reconstruct our nation. But in all this, we do not need to fear, for God remains enthroned in heaven, and He will move, remove, and alter the leaders, governments, and powers of nations according to His divine purpose. History is neither cyclical nor haphazard. Instead, it is ultimately linear, controlled, and directed by a sovereign God who moves all nations toward His predetermined outcome: when Christ will usher in His kingdom and establish His eternal reign. Because of His activity, we do not need to fear who is elected or what changes will happen in our society. God is in control, and that is sufficient for us.

Day 4
The Sovereignty of God: The Audacity of Man

Read Romans 9:6–26

Who are you, O man, who answers back to God?
Romans 9:20

Theologians struggle to fully understand God's sovereign work concerning free will as Paul discusses the operation of God's sovereignty in human history. In discussing the outworking of God's redemptive plan, Paul points out that Jacob's selection over Esau was based upon God's redemptive promise rather than on any intrinsic worth of Jacob over Esau. It was grounded solely in God's sovereign purpose. However, this is not just seen in the selection of Jacob but also in God's activity throughout Israel's history. For example, while showing mercy to Israel, God hardened Pharaoh's heart to remain unmoved by Moses's appeal. The result was that Israel was delivered while Pharaoh and his armies were destroyed. Naturally, this raises an objection that God is unjust in showing favor to one over the other. If God is just, how can he show mercy to some and bring judgment upon others?

To answer the question, Paul does not delve into an in-depth theological or philosophical discussion regarding God's sovereignty and the interplay it has with our freedom of will. Instead, he goes to the heart of the issue and addresses the real question: does God have the right to exercise His sovereignty as He pleases, or is He accountable to us? Just as we find in Ephesians 1, so also here, amid the debate, we can lose the forest for the trees. To understand and worship God for His sovereignty, we need to come to grips with the reality that God is God, and we are not.

Just as the clay does not have the right to tell the potter what to make, so we do not have the right to question God and tell Him what He can and cannot do. God exercises His sovereignty according to His purpose, not according to our wishes or mandates. We want a God who is sovereign, but only in the areas we want. He can do as He pleases—as long as He acts in a way consistent with what we want or desire.

This is the audacity of humanity: we want the freedom to determine our destinies and govern our own lives. We make our plans, set our goals, plot out the paths of our lives, and then ask God to bless them. When He interrupts our lives, when His Word conflicts with our desires and perspectives, when He sovereignly changes the course we chose by interposing life-altering circumstances, we question God and find fault with Him. Nevertheless, God is not an all-powerful God who exists merely to respond to our bidding. He is a sovereign God, enthroned in heaven, who directs the universe and our lives to achieve His intentions. His goal is not to do what pleases us but to reveal the riches of His glory by demonstrating His patience (Romans 9:22).

It is one thing to affirm His sovereignty when He acts in ways consistent with our plans. It is quite another to accept His control when He works contrary to our goals. To learn to rest in the comfort of His sovereignty, we must recognize His right to do as He pleases in our lives. This rest comes when we completely surrender to His sovereign activity.

To affirm His position as the sovereign King is to humble yourself before Him, to place yourself in complete submission to His will. If God is truly sovereign, governed by His love, empowered by His omnipotence, acting according to His infinite knowledge and wisdom, then the only proper response is to relinquish the pursuit of your will and submit to His. Anything less is to attempt to usurp His position as the universal King. Today, ask God to ultimately impose His will upon yours, to enable you to allow Him to guide your footsteps without question and to find complete joy in fulfilling His purpose.

Day 5
The Sovereignty of God: Trusting God When We Do Not Know the Future

Read Daniel 3

If it be so, our God whom we serve is able to deliver us from the furnace of blazing fire . . . but even if He does not . . . we are not going to serve your gods.
Daniel 3:17

No one likes to be different or to stand out in the crowd. There is something inherent within us that desires to conform to the masses. So, it is easy for us to understand the pressure confronting Shadrach, Meshack, and Abed-nego. In an act of extreme arrogance, Nebuchadnezzar made an image of himself and commanded every person in the whole kingdom to bow down and acknowledge their allegiance to him and worship him as a god. As the music began to play, one can imagine the scene as all the assembled multitudes bowed in unison to the golden image that stood ninety feet high. But amid the crowd, three men remained standing. As they looked about them, all their friends and relatives, all the Jews that had been gathered, were bowing. The pressure to conform would have been unbearable. However, that was the least of their worries. In their act of non-conformity, they were committing treason, for they were in direct defiance of the king's order, and their actions would have been viewed as a rejection of his authority. Nebuchadnezzar's response was quick and predictable. In the face of such rebellion, Nebuchadnezzar brought them before him and gave them an ultimatum: either affirm their loyalty by submitting to the command to worship him or face a horrible death in a burning furnace.

Shadrach, Meshack, and Abed-nego had already counted the cost and agreed upon their response. They stood tall and firm. Yet, their response gives us insight into the meaning of living and resting in the sovereignty of God. In their statement (Daniel 3:17–18), they highlight two important truths. First, that God has the ability to save them even from the power of a king. The God who delivered Israel from Egypt, the one who divided the seas and established the nation, is a God who is more significant than any earthly leader.

Second, they trusted in the sovereign plan of God. While God certainly had the power and ability to deliver them, they accepted that His sovereign plan might include them perishing at the hands of this pagan king. In humble submission, they accepted the fact that God does not deliver His people from every hardship. His plan, which is unseen by us, may involve suffering and even death.

This is an essential lesson in trusting in the sovereignty of God. Nothing is haphazard with God. But this does not mean God will deliver us from every one of our problems and trials. In His infinite wisdom, He may allow us to face tragedy and struggles to achieve a deeper purpose. We do not always understand why He allows things to happen, but He asks us to simply trust Him, even when His plan is unclear. Throughout history, God has allowed many of His followers to experience tragic death. This does not mean God failed, only that God has a different purpose. Just because God can deliver us does not mean that He will.

Nevertheless, in the end, the outcome is already assured by a sovereign God. He promises He will always be with you in every circumstance, and He has promised you eternal life in Him, and nothing can threaten or thwart His promise. His sovereignty assures you that your eternal life is never threatened. Thus, in the uncertainty of the day, you can trust in God's sovereign plan, a plan that does not guarantee you freedom from trials and even death, but a plan that assures you of your final victory over suffering and death.

The Providence of God

For as the rain and the snow come down from heaven, and do not return there without watering the earth and making it produce and sprout, and providing seed to the sower and bread to the eater, so is my word that goes out from my mouth.
Isaiah 55:10

Closely related to the sovereignty of God is His providential care of creation. When we are going through difficulties and times of uncertainty, we struggle to find contentment. While we affirm His sovereignty, we can doubt whether God is indifferent to our plight. Such was the struggle that Job faced. As Job struggled to comprehend the disaster that descended upon him, he could not understand why heaven seemed silent. If God was sovereign, then why did He not act on Job's behalf? Instead of God bringing deliverance, it seemed as if God had turned away with indifference (see Job 30:16–21). Instead of His sovereignty being a source of comfort, it became a mockery.

To have a proper perspective of God's sovereignty, we must also understand His providence. God's providence refers to that aspect of His nature that moves God to care and provide for His creation continually. His providence means that He is not indifferent to His people's needs but actively engaged in providing for them and for all creation. In Colossians 1:17, we are reminded that "He is before all things and in Him, all things hold together." So also in Hebrews 1:3, we find that Christ upholds all things by the word of His power.

In Matthew 6:25–34, Christ establishes the providential care of God. The assurance this gives provides us with the foundation we need to no longer be anxious when adversity threatens us. When our world seems to be falling apart around us, anxiety grips our thoughts and emotions. Throughout history, humanity has viewed wealth as the means for security in life. Nevertheless, wealth is an illusion; it makes a promise that it cannot keep, for it does not provide any lasting refuge. In the end, materialism clouds our perspective of life and distorts our priorities. Rather than alleviating our fears, it only adds to them as we become anxious about our financial stability.

Instead of turning to wealth to provide for our needs, Christ points us back to God. Christ mentions the three foundational needs we have for life: the need for adequate food, water, and protection from the elements. However, He moves our attention away from these to point out that we have an even more basic need—the need for God. Our security in life is not found in ourselves, our abilities, our finances, or our control of our circumstances, but in the providential care of God. Christ makes this point by comparing our value to that of the birds of the air. They do nothing to provide for their well-being, yet God superabundantly cares for them. If God cares so much for a relatively insignificant creature, how much more will God care for we who are created in His image and who stand as the pinnacle of His creative work! If our security and life come from God, who is infinite in His resources and power, then we no longer need to fear. As Isaiah reminds us, "Do not fear, for I have redeemed you; I have called you by name, you are Mine! When you pass through the waters, I will be with you; and through the rivers, they will not overflow you. When you walk through the fire, you will not be scorched, nor the flame burn you" (Isaiah 43:1–2). God will not forget us! God knows our needs, and He acts to meet those needs.

Considering God's providential care, you are to have a different perspective of life. Instead of being occupied with attaining the world's things, you are now free to focus on the pursuit of God's kingdom, His righteousness, and His will. Instead of worrying about the future and the security you will have, you can trust God to care for you. Consequently, you can now live in the present, serving Him.

Day 1
The Providence of God: Christ Upholds All Things

Read Colossians 1:15–20

He is before all things, and in Him, all things hold together. Colossians 1:17

Colossians 1:15–20 is regarded by many to be one of the greatest hymns and celebrations of the person of Christ found in the whole New Testament. In just a few sentences, Paul captures Christ's divine nature, preeminence, and redemptive work. Verse 15 captures the divine essence He shares with the Father. Christ is the perfect representation of God, for He is God Himself. Paul then points out that when God spoke the universe into existence, it was accomplished through the person of Christ, who was the Word of God (John 1:1). Because of this, He is the firstborn of all creation (v. 15). This does not mean that He was the first created being, as some have suggested. The term "firstborn," which draws its metaphorical significance from the Old Testament, refers to the one in the highest position of preeminence in the family, the one through whom the family name and heritage would proceed. The priority of Christ is further highlighted in verse 16 when Paul celebrates that Christ stands above and over all creation; not only does the universe owe its existence to Christ, but Christ is the goal of creation ("for Him"). In other words, Christ stands at the beginning of creation and He stands at the end, or as the goal, of creation.

In verse 17, Paul carries it a step further when he states that Christ is also the one who sustains creation. From beginning to end and everywhere in the middle, Christ gives life, purpose, and meaning to the whole universe. The word "hold" speaks of one who maintains many parts as a cohesive and enduring whole. This is further emphasized in the tense of the verb, which suggests continual and constant cohesions. In other words, Christ is the glue that holds the universe together. Science has long been baffled by understanding what binds together the fundamental forces of nature (i.e., matter, radiation, forces, space, and time). Einstein believed that if we probed the essence of physics deeply enough, there would be one and only one way that everything works together. In the quest to discover this unifying principle, some proposed that the universe is held together by tiny vibrating strings. However, Paul gives us the answer that has mystified quantum physics. The unifying force binding all things together is not just some impersonal scientific law; it is a living person, Christ himself.

Because a person, rather than an impersonal force, binds the universe together, we discover meaning, purpose, and design in all things. Furthermore, because an omnipotent God is sustaining the universe, we do not fear the collapse of the universe, for its sustainability depends not on man but God.

What is true of the universe is equally valid for our individual lives as well. Christ is not only the sustainer of the universe, but

He is also the sustainer of our own lives. In a world of chaotic chance, Christ is the one who brings cohesion and meaning. At times, especially in times of difficulty, life can seem out of control, lacking purpose and security. However, we can trust in Christ's providential hand. When we speak of the providence of God, we are affirming God's presence in the universe whereby He upholds and preserves all things and governs all things by His purpose. The existence of the world and universe is not grounded in chance or even in man's ability, but in God's involvement in creation, whereby He sustains all things and moves all things to fulfill His purpose.

When life becomes confusing, you have the assurance of God's supporting hand. Your life is not determined by chance or by the "miracles of modern medicine." Instead, your life is governed by the providential care of a loving God.

Day 2
The Providence of God Demonstrated in the Life of Israel

Read Deuteronomy 29:2–9

I have led you forty years in the wilderness; your clothes have not worn out on you . . . so that you might know that I am the LORD your God. Deuteronomy 29:5

Forty years is a long time to march in the wilderness. The land where Israel wandered was a barren wasteland devoid of any resources. It remains a land where the struggle for survival would be difficult for a Bedouin family but impossible for a whole tribe, numbering between one and a half to three million people. There were no stores to purchase supplies; no Amazon to call up for home delivery when things ran out. It was a land where daily existence would be a struggle for survival.

Nevertheless, their struggle was a result of their own choices and sin. God's purpose was to bring them into the promised land, a land "flowing with milk and honey." However, fear, rather than faith, dictated their actions. Instead of trusting in God's promise, the Israelites became fearful of the armies of the inhabitants. As a result, they refused to follow God's command to enter the land. Because of their unbelief, God disciplined them by forcing them to spend the next forty years in a land that was just the opposite of what He had promised. Instead of a land flowing with milk and honey, they were forced to live in a land of rocks and heat, where food would be scarce, water challenging to find, and survival a daily challenge.

Most remarkable about the story is not the discipline and judgment of God but rather His providential care for Israel throughout their wilderness wandering. During their time in the wilderness, God continued to provide for their needs. Soon after Israel had left Egypt, God supplied their requirements by supernaturally providing manna for their daily provision of food. When the people became tired of the manna and grumbled against Moses and even God, God patiently and graciously provided meat for them to eat. It was not until they entered the promised land, celebrated their first Passover, and enjoyed their first meal of the produce from the land that the manna ceased (Joshua 5:10–12). For over forty years, God had providentially provided for their needs. So caring was God for Israel's needs, even after they had disobeyed and suffered His discipline, that their clothes did not wear out and the shoes they wore daily showed no signs of decay.

It is one thing for God in His providence to care for our needs when we are walking in fellowship and obedience; it is quite another for Him to care for us even when we rebel. But God's providential care extends to all people, even those disobeying him. Christ reminds us of God's providential care in the Sermon on the Mount, "For He causes His sun to rise on the evil and the good, and sends rain on the righteous and the unrighteous" (Matthew 5:45). God, in the wonder of His grace, sustains all people, not just the righteous.

When we face adversity in life, it is easy to become anxious about God's care for us, especially when our suffering results from our own decisions to live independently of God. We begin to be fearful of His goodness. In 1 Corinthians 10:1–13, Paul refers to Israel's deliverance and discipline as an example of our own need to live in obedience to God. It also serves as an example of God's gracious provision even when we do not deserve it. Regardless of why we are suffering (whether it be because of our sin, the sin of others, the fact that we live in a fallen world, or God's desire to display his glory), we have assurance that God will still provide for us. Instead of doubting God's care when trials come your way, look for ways in which God is demonstrating His grace by providing for your needs and then thank and praise Him for His providence.

Day 3
The Providence of God: God Knows Our Needs and Responds to Our Prayers

Read Matthew 6:7–15

For your Father knows what you need before you ask Him. Matthew 6:8

The English word *providence* comes from the Greek word *pro-noia*, which is a combination of two words: the Greek preposition *pro* (which means "before") and the word *nous*. The word *nous* means "knowledge, disposition, or a particular way of thinking." Thus, the word means to "to take thought beforehand, give attention to," with the implication of responding appropriately to a need. The word *therefore* points to God's foresight, or making provision beforehand for our needs. While the word itself does not occur in our passage, the concept of God's providential care is wonderfully illustrated and highlighted.

The passage begins with a warning against meaningless prayer. The term translated as "meaningless repetition" is a word from which we derive our English word *babble*. In other words, Christ exhorts us not to "babble" in our prayers. For many, the way to be heard by the gods was to make long, repetitive prayers that would sound more impressive and thus elicit a response from the deity. In some ways, we can fall into the same trap, especially in public prayers. Sometimes we think the more eloquent our prayer, the longer we pray, and the more we repeat the prayer, the greater the chance that God will listen and respond. While God encourages us to be persistent in prayer (see Luke 18:1), the reason is to test our resolve in trusting God, not to try to motivate an indifferent God to somehow respond to our request.

The reason we are not to be like the babblers is our understanding of the providence of God. God already knows our prayer even before we ask. However, here we must take careful note of the words of Scripture. Christ does not say merely that God knows our needs, but that He knows our needs *in advance*. In other words, before we even identify a need as significant enough to warrant us seeking help from God, God is already fully aware of it. The implication of this goes beyond mere knowledge. Christ is making the point that our heavenly Father is already motivated and moving to respond to our request before we even know we have a need. This is what we often fail to understand about prayer. We often view prayer as the means of informing God of what He does not know so that He might act in a way differently than He currently is.

Consequently, we believe we need to be articulate in prayer so that God will understand what He needs to do. Yet that misses the whole purpose. Christ's point is that we have assurance that God, in His providence, knows and acts on our behalf before we even have a need. Therefore, our prayer no longer needs to focus upon what we need but can instead concentrate on the pursuit of God and His purpose for us, which is at the heart of the Lord's Prayer. In terms of Christ's teaching on prayer, the focus is not upon what we need (as is often the case in our prayers) but upon God's will and the goal of a life of obedience to him. Instead of being anxious about our daily struggles in life (Matthew 6:15–32), we can focus on seeking His righteousness.

As we face trials in life, we quickly can become distracted by them. We become focused on the problem and on seeking God's intervention. However, the promise of providential care assures us that He is already acting on our behalf, so we can remain focused on what is truly important—attaining His righteousness and fulfilling His will. Therefore, even as you ask for God's help in the present struggle, keep your focus on what is truly important. Instead of just praying for His deliverance, pray for wisdom to do His will and to reveal Him to others during your crisis.

Day 4
God's Providence Gives Us Confidence in the Face of Threats

Read 2 Samuel 10:9–14

May the LORD do what is good in His sight. 2 Samuel 10:12

In a surprising twist, the only words about trusting in God in this chapter do not come from the lips of David. In the next chapter, we find David beginning to decline as a leader as he neglects his kingly responsibility to lead his people into battle. This would eventually lead to David's moral and spiritual failure when he commits adultery with Bathsheba and then seeks to cover his sin with the murder of her husband. Therefore, it is not surprising that the expression of faith is not found on his lips but on the lips of his generals.

In 2 Samuel 10, we find the Ammonites rejecting David's gesture of peace. Rather than accepting the gesture, the new king, Hanun, humiliated the messengers of David by shaving half their beards and cutting off their garments in the middle of their hips. This cultural humiliation soon turned into a threat of war as Ammon, joined by the Arameans, marshaled its troops for battle. When David heard of it, he sent Joab to lead his armies to fight against them rather than going out himself.

Facing the formidable threat of two armies, Joab split his forces, placing half under his command and the other half under Abishai's control. Even then, Joab recognized that the forces arrayed against him might be too great. Defeat appeared imminent. In response, Joab makes the only direct reference to God in the chapter—and what he says governs the whole episode. When confronted with the threat before him, Joab assures Abishai of the providential care of God: "May the LORD do what is good in His sight" (v. 12). These words expressed his faith that God is good and will care for His people. But in his statement, there is also faith and surrender to the purposes of God, to the belief that God is the one who decides the outcome and what is right, not us. This expression is not just a hope that God will do what is good, but that God Himself is the one who determines what is right. Trusting in the providence of God is trusting that God not only preserves and cares for us and orders everything according to what is good, but that He also determines what is good.

This surrender to God's will is what makes Joab's statement so remarkable. Joab was confident in God and fully trusted God with the outcome, no matter what the result might be. It is one thing to trust God when things come up smelling like roses; it is quite another to trust Him in the face of possible death. Yet, this is the essence of faith. Because God cares for us, we can trust Him no matter what enemy we face. He cares for us in any situation or threat, providing us the strength we need. As we walk dependent upon God and doing His will, He gives us power surpassing the struggles we face. The outcome may be different than what we want or expect, but we have assurance that the results will be profitable based on God's perspective, not ours. Too often, in times of trial, we pray for God to do what is good in our sight. Instead, we need to pray for Him to do what is good in His perspective. Our view is limited and faulty; His sight is eternal and perfect.

Today, as you bring your struggles before the presence of God, rest in His providential care and trust that He is infinitely wiser in determining what is good and right.

Day 5
The Providence of God: God Supplies All Our Needs

Read Philippians 4:10–20

My God will supply all your needs according to His riches in glory in Christ Jesus. Philippians 4:19

Perhaps the most difficult attitude to cultivate in our lives is an attitude of contentment that overflows into an attitude of giving rather than hoarding and saving. Contentment comes when we trust God to provide all we need both in the present and in the future. Because we have that assurance, we are now free to give generously to the needs of others for we no longer fear the future. In the closing words of Paul's letter to the church at Philippi, Paul examines these two qualities. In Philippians 4:11–13, Paul affirms that he has learned to be content in whatever circumstance he encounters. Paul realized that contentment is not a natural character quality but one cultivated and developed through the Holy Spirit's sanctifying work. In his classic book, *The Rare Jewel of Christian Contentment*, puritan Jeremiah Burroughs (1599–1646) described Christian contentment as "that sweet, inward, quiet, gracious frame of spirit, which freely submits to and delights in God's wise and fatherly disposal in every condition."[11] For Paul, the secret to learning to be content in every circumstance came from his understanding that God provided for all his needs and strengthened him to face any occasion. Thus, Burroughs points out, "My brethren, the reason why you have not got contentment in the things of the world is not that

---

11. Jeremiah Burroughs, *The Rare Jewel of Christian Contentment* (Edinburgh: The Banner of Truth Trust, 1992), 40.

you have not got enough of them. That is not the reason. But the reason is that they are not things proportionable to that immortal soul of yours that is capable of God himself."[12] Contentment comes when we realize that all we need is what God provides, and what He has provided is Himself.

Now we come to the second theme of this passage. Paul commends the church at Philippi for their willingness to share in his ministry by providing financial support. Even though Paul had established several churches in Asia Minor, only the church at Philippi "shared with me in the matter of giving and receiving" (v. 15). Why were the people at Philippi so giving when all the other churches were self-absorbed and tightfisted? The answer lies in verse 19. They recognized that God supplied all their needs according to His riches. Just as the providential care of God brought a spirit of contentment to Paul, so the awareness of His care provided the church with the confidence to share in the needs of others, even when they themselves were lacking. When Paul mentions the churches of Macedonia who gave "in a great ordeal of affliction and . . . their deep poverty" (2 Corinthians 8:2), he likely had the Philippians primarily in mind. Concerning the relationship of giving and the providence of God, Burroughs writes, "Nothing befalls you, good or evil, but there is a providence in those things that is of the infinite and eternal God."[13]

To trust in God's providence is to rest in the provision of God altogether. Because He cares for us, He gives us all we need, so we require nothing more. Contentment does not come when satisfied with what we have; it is satisfied with what God has given us. This comes when we realize that God has given us the greatest need of all—the need of Him. Paul reminds us that our ultimate need is that which only Christ can provide. If we are without Christ, no number of earthly possessions will be adequate; if we have Christ, there is no need for any other possession. Therefore,

---

12. Ibid, 91.
13. Ibid, 112.

when you find yourself dissatisfied, the answer is not found in the pursuit of more things but in the pursuit of a deeper relationship with Christ.

The Jealousy and Wrath of God

For behold, the LORD will come in fire and His chariots like the whirlwind, to render His anger with fury, and His rebuke with flames of fire.
Isaiah 66:15

We focus on the love of God but ignore the warnings of His wrath. We want a God who does not take sin seriously, who does not bring judgment—and if He does, it is only temporary. Consequently, we view hell not as a place of eternal punishment but as a temporary place for people to finally come to realize God's grace. However, this fails to recognize that in Scripture, God is both a God of love and a God of jealousy and wrath. If we understand His entire character, we must also affirm that He is a God who is zealous for His righteousness. In Nahum 1:2, we find three statements that provide a perspective of His wrath.

First, God is a jealous God. Often, the word jealousy has a negative connotation in our minds. Yet, in Scripture, we also find a positive meaning of the word. In Song of Solomon 8:6, in celebrating the virtues and strength of love, the bride asks her husband to "put me like a seal over your heart, like a seal on your arm for love is as strong as death, jealousy is as severe as Sheol." Here jealousy is not the controlling, possessive love we often identify, but the desire for an exclusive relationship with no rival, no divided loyalty. In other words, this jealousy is a deep commitment to honor and protect a relationship against all intrusions that would harm it. Such is the nature of God. When the Bible speaks of God as a jealous God, it refers to His deep zeal to protect His love relationship with His people. He does not allow for divided loyalties. This is why idolatry is so abhorrent to God. God does not allow for anything to undermine His relationship with His people.

Second, God is an avenging God. Like the word jealousy, we often view the idea of God being an avenging God as somehow unfitting to His character. Yet, for a holy and pure God, any sin is an insult to His nature. Sin involves a rejection of Him, and thus His justice demands that a penalty be enacted. God cannot be true to His holiness and righteousness if He allows sin and rebellion to go unchecked and unpunished, for to do so would destroy any and every relationship He has with His people. Thus, the vengeance of God is interwoven with His justice and salvation. To carry out vengeance, one must have the proper authority to do so. This is why only God can bring judgment. Only God is King, and only He is righteous, so only He has the power and standard to enforce what is right. But this is balanced by the greatness of His mercy. His justice demands the judgment of sin, but His mercy provides the opportunity for His verdict to be averted. He is not only the God of wrath; He is also the God of mercy.

Third, God is a God of wrath. The wrath of God refers to His resolve to punish sin. God cannot be good and righteous if He tolerates and accepts evil. If God loves all that is good and righteous, it follows that He must equally hate all that is evil and immoral. Central to both the Old and New Testaments is the teaching that God will judge sin. Christ, in Matthew 10:34, warns, "Do not think that I came to bring peace on the earth; I did not come to bring peace, but a sword." This is fully realized at the end of the age which Christ returns to bring swift and severe judgment upon the sinful world (see the book of Revelation.)

His wrath is also interwoven with His grace. While God will judge sinners with eternal judgment, He offers a way of escape. Because of Christ's work on the cross, when Christ took upon Himself the retribution we deserved because of our sin, He made it possible for us to be free from God's judgment.

When we contemplate His wrath, it should lead to four critical applications. First, just as we worship God for His mercy, we should equally worship Him for His righteous indignation. Second, we must recognize that He does not allow anything to come between Himself and His people because He is a jealous God. God loves us and bestows upon us His complete and unyielding loyalty, and He desires us to express the same fidelity to Him. Third, to be like Christ, we should share His hatred of evil, injustice, and sin. While we must love the sinner even as Christ loves the sinner, it is never loving to become complacent toward sin. Sin is always destructive in the lives of people. To treat sin lightly or excuse sin in others is never loving, for it is to be indifferent to their spiritual condition. Fourth, it fails to recognize that sin results in the judgment of eternal punishment. To hate sin and love the sinner moves us to share with them the hope of the gospel. Last, this gives us hope in times of adversity. The wrath of God provides us the assurance that sin and its destructive effects will not always win the day. There will come a time when God deals with sin and restores righteousness, peace, and freedom.

Day 1
The Jealousy of God: God Is Jealous for His Glory

Read Exodus 20:1–17

You shall have no other gods before Me. Exodus 20:3

When we think of the word jealousy, we often think of the term negatively—of the controlling and overly possessive control of another person. However, there is also a positive perspective of jealousy. Positively, jealousy involves being vigilant in maintaining and protecting a relationship. The Oxford Dictionary describes it as "being fiercely protective or vigilant of one's rights or possessions."[14] In this sense, the Bible speaks of God's jealousy, namely, that He is fiercely protective of His reputation and honor.

In Isaiah 48:11, God says, "For My own sake, for My own sake, I will act; for how can My name be profaned? And My glory I will not give to another." At first glance, it seems troubling to us that God would jealously protect His honor. This stems from our sense of pride. We are wrongly jealous of our honor and glory for the simple reason that, in the end, we are corrupt and sinful, where our sinful nature taints every thought and action. Our jealousy for our glory is grounded in greed and covetousness. We want the praise that we do not deserve since only God is holy, perfect, and worthy of honor (Revelation 4:11).

Because God alone is wholly righteous and worthy of all honor and His character is morally right and pure, His reputation and integrity are precious. For us to think otherwise would imply that God is sinful and imperfect. Therefore, He is intensely

---

14. https://www.lexico.com/en/definition/jealous, Accessed 8/28/2021

jealous and protective of His glory and honor. To share His glory with any other person or being is to make the other equal with God and thus a rival to God.

This brings us back to the seriousness of sin, for at the heart of all evil is a rejection of God. Because God is undefiled by sin and is holy, God cannot tolerate any sin, no matter how small or insignificant. When God condemns sin, it is because He is holy. Thus, He reacts in wrath, for it is an insult to Him and His desire that only what is right and good be revealed. A world that celebrates sin and normalizes immorality stands in complete repudiation of who God is. To accept and tolerate sin is to reject and devalue God and arouse His jealous anger.

To truly love God is to be jealous for His character, glory, and reputation in every circumstance we face in life. To be jealous for God's glory is to live to please Him and reveal His character and goodness to the world. When we face trials, it often reveals our focus. Is it upon ourselves—our reputations, successes, and glories—or is it upon God and showing Him to our world? We are to obey His commands, avoid any association with other religions, and remain loyal only to Him and His character. To be jealous for God is to strive to please Him in everything and reveal His goodness in all our actions. To be jealous for God is to hate sin (not the sinner) in all its forms and to live to reveal Him in all that we do. Anything less is an invitation for His wrath. Today, look at your actions and ask yourself, "Am I manifesting Christ's goodness and purity in all that I do and think?"

Day 2
The Jealousy of God: God Desires Our Complete Devotion

Deuteronomy 5:1–21

You shall not worship them or serve them; for I, the LORD *your God, am a jealous God.* Deuteronomy 5:9

The Ten Commandments have long been cherished for their brevity and the scope of their coverage. In these few statements, God establishes the moral, ethical, and religious foundation for a society to flourish and succeed. In Deuteronomy 5, God again graciously offers the people of Israel the opportunity to enter a binding relationship with Him. If they are willing to do so, He will be their God, and He will bless them and protect them, giving them the promised land as their inheritance. First, however, as their king, God sets forth what He requires of them in the Ten Commandments. These commandments provide the bedrock of living in His kingdom, encompassing both their relationship with Him and how they are to relate to one another. Christ would later sum up these commands (and all the moral, ethical, and religious commands of the Bible) with two brief statements: We are to love the Lord our God, and we are to love our neighbor as ourselves.

At the center of the commandments is the fidelity we are to demonstrate to Him as our king. Just as a citizen cannot pledge allegiance to two different kings, so God requires that we give Him our complete devotion. To have other gods, to form idols, or to worship another would be a violation of our loyalty. Consequently, He reminds us that He is a jealous God. When

God established a covenant with His people through the Mosaic covenant, and when He established a covenant with us through the new covenant, He affirmed His loyalty. He will never fail to protect and provide for us. We can trust in Him completely.

God desires an exclusive relationship that has no rivals, one grounded in complete fidelity. His covenant with us also places upon us the responsibility of jealously protecting our relationship with Him and being whole loyal to Him. God expects us to love Him in return. This love is more than an emotional response; it is a structured relationship that demonstrates our loyalty through our obedience. When adversity strikes in our life, it serves to strip away what is unimportant and a distraction. It reminds us that people and relationships are far more critical than accomplishments and possessions. The same is true of our relationship with God. At the end of life, only one thing truly matters: have we maintained our fidelity to God? It is easy in life to allow many different "idols" to intrude in our relationship with God: work, hobbies, the pursuit of success, the pursuit of wealth, pleasure, the philosophy of the world, and the list could go on. When we face trials, it provides us an opportunity to assess our lives and priorities and ask ourselves, "Is God first in my life?"

Day 3
God's Wrath Reveals the Severity and Destruction of Sin

Read Romans 1:18–32

For the wrath of God is revealed from heaven against all ungodliness. Romans 1:18

Just as God's love is demonstrated in His grace toward us, so also His holiness, by necessity, must be revealed in the outpouring of His wrath upon sin. Yet, somehow, we find His indignation objectionable. We want a loving God who accepts all people regardless of their sin or rejection of Him, but we do not want a God who will punish sin and judge evil.

Nevertheless, God does not give us this choice. To accept some attributes (His love, peace, and righteousness) while denying others (such as His justice and wrath) is to deny God the intrinsic qualities of His nature. In the end, it is to recreate God into an idol. As Stephen Charnock points out in his classic work, *The Existence and Attributes of God*, "There is something of a secret atheism in all, which is the foundation of the evil practices in their lives, not an utter disowning of the being of God, but a denial or doubting of some of the rights of his nature."[15] He goes on to state, "The absolute disowning of the being of God is not natural to men, but the contrary is natural; but an inconsideration of God, or misrepresentation of his nature, is natural to man as corrupt."[16] This is revealed in our attempt to deny that God will pour out His righteous anger upon sin.

On almost every page in Scripture, we see the warning that to ignore God's moral standard of holiness in thought, conduct, and morality is to invite His wrath and judgment upon us. This is what Paul warns in Romans 1. To accept, tolerate, or promote any sin is to ultimately deny God His essential righteousness and embrace idolatry, for an idol is not just the worship of another god, but the denial of any character quality of God. However, this takes us back to the garden of Eden. When Adam and Eve ate the forbidden fruit, it was not just a simple act of disobedience. It was the attempt to throw off the constraints of God's holy standard in order to pursue life independent of God. The desire "to

---

15. Steven Charnock, *The Existence and Attributes of God*, vol. 1 (Grand Rapids: Baker Book House, 1981), 24.

16. Ibid, 25.

be like God, knowing good and evil" (Genesis 3:5) was humanity's attempt to become masters of our destiny and to determine our own morality. This is now finding expression in our pursuit of sexual immorality (vv. 26–27), greed (v. 28), hatred of others (v. 29), and selfish pride (v. 30). However, in the end, it becomes the lie of Satan in the garden, for instead of bringing freedom, it brings enslavement to sin.

Within Scripture, we discover two ways that God's wrath is realized. First, as we see in this chapter, we see God's judgment in removing His restraint of sin so that people are given over to the bondage of their immorality and destructive behavior. Second, as we see in the book of Revelation, God's wrath is revealed in His final and eternal punishment of sin and of those who reject him.

All this points to the importance of not only accepting God in the totality of His being but also taking sin and its effects in our lives seriously. To excuse or overlook sin in our lives only brings disastrous results, both in our own lives and in our relationship with God. Therefore, when we are aware of its presence, we must respond with repentance, turning from our sin to pursue the path of righteousness. But, of course, to practice righteousness begins with recognizing God's hatred of sin, for only then will we understand and pursue the offer of His grace.

Day 4
The Wrath of God: The Offer of Grace

Read John 3:16–36

He who believes in the Son has eternal life; but he who does not obey the Son will not see life, but the wrath of God abides on him. John 3:36

Charles Dickens, in *A Tale of Two Cities*, opens with a classic line, "It was the best of times, it was the worst of times, it was the age of wisdom, it was the age of foolishness, it was the epoch of belief, it was the epoch of incredulity, it was the season of Light, it was the season of Darkness, it was the spring of hope, it was the winter of despair, we had everything before us, we had nothing before us, we were all going direct to Heaven, we were all going direct the other way . . ."[17] In this line, Dickens sets the tone for the book as he wrestles with the contrasts of extremes that exemplified the time of the French Revolution.

These words also serve to echo the contrasting choice we find in John 3. Eternal life comes down to a simple choice between two opposing options. To accept by faith the redemptive work of Christ and submit to Him brings eternal life; to reject the offer is to experience God's wrath. What is important to realize is that the basis for the two choices and outcomes is not grounded in our efforts or in any inherent goodness within us; rather, it is grounded in the simple act of faith. Christ makes it clear that all religious paths do not lead to the same location. Instead, Christ reduces the paths of faith to two elementary roads.

---

17. Charles Dickens, *A Tale of Two Cities*, https://www.gutenberg.org/files/98/old/2city12p.pdf, 4, accessed 8/30/2021.

The first road is those who believe in Christ and accept His redemptive work on the cross. For those who chose to follow this path, their eternal destiny is assured, for they obtain eternal life (vv. 16, 18a). Those who walk this road recognize their spiritual need, understanding that sin separates them from God, and they need someone to restore their relationship with Christ. That mediator is Christ Himself, for He became our substitute by taking upon Himself the penalty for sin that a just and holy God requires.

The other road, encompassing all other religions and paths, is a road grounded in rejection and unbelief. Those walking this path are not simply facing the prospect of judgment but are already judged, for they have already been condemned as lawbreakers. Those who walk this path are revealed by how they live, for they live in disobedience to Christ. Instead of surrendering to Christ, they chose to live their lives completely independent of Christ. Rather than submitting, they defiantly reject God's word and His commands. Rather than coming to Christ, they fear that their sin will be exposed, so they flee from Him (vv. 19–20). They may be religious, even claiming to be Christian, but in the end, their religion is powerless and devoid of any genuine and lasting life change. They are the individuals Christ warns in Matthew 7:21–23: "Not everyone who says to Me, 'Lord, Lord,' will enter the kingdom of heaven, but he who does the will of My Father who is in heaven will enter" (Matthew 7:21). In other words, our obedience and actions reveal the authenticity of our faith.

This is what brings us back to our understanding of God's wrath and His utter hatred of sin. Only when we see the reality of God's wrath upon sin can we know the wonder of His grace and the beauty of the offer of Christ's salvation. Salvation does not come from the denial of His wrath but the understanding that His wrath was fully satisfied by the work of Christ on the cross. Only when we understand God's wrath can we truly understand our need for salvation. Thus, we are left with a decision regarding which road we are going to travel. The way of surrender and acceptance of Christ leads to life. The route of self-determination and rejection of Christ leads to death. Which path have you chosen?

Day 5
The Wrath of God: The Comfort of the Believer

Read Revelation 22:1–15

Blessed is he who heeds the words of the prophecy of this book. Revelation 22:7

For some, the book of Revelation is perhaps the most terrifying and foreboding book in all of Scripture. Some argue that the picture of God in the Old Testament is a God of wrath and judgment, while the God of the New Testament (mainly seen in the person of Christ) is a God of love and compassion who accepts all people. However, the book of Revelation dispels this theory, for it presents the second coming of Christ as a time of the final outpouring of God's wrath and judgment upon sin. In a crescendo of retributions that are both frightening in severity and universal in scope, the appearance of Christ brings the final condemnation of Satan, his demons, and all those who have rejected the salvation of Christ as He casts them into the eternal lake of fire (Revelation 20:13–15).

With such a dark mood throughout the book, it is surprising that the book's purpose is to be a source of blessing for God's people. How can the most remarkable display of God's wrath in all of Scripture be a blessing? To understand this, we must place God's wrath in the context of His justice.

Justice demands retribution against all unrighteousness. A wave of righteous anger is aroused when we see businesses forced to close because the owner strives to follow biblical principles; when there is a blatant abuse of power; when racism continues to be rampant; when the murder of infants remains unchecked; when immorality is promoted even to children. My mother said many years ago that we live in an "Alice in Wonderland world," where wrong has become right and right has become wrong. She would be shocked to see how prophetic her words turned out to be. If our anger is not aroused when we see unrighteousness prevail and realize the damage it causes then there is something wrong, for to be angry over sin is an expression of God's righteousness. Psalm 7:11 states, "God is a righteous judge, and a God who has indignation every day."

This justice of God is the source of our blessing. Indeed, we do not find joy in the eternal judgment of sinners, for even though God will judge, the Bible states that He takes no pleasure in the death of the wicked but desires all people to repent and receive salvation (Ezekiel 33:11). Thus, the source of blessing is found in restoring all that is just and right and holy and removing evil and those that promote it.

Therefore, for the Christian, the message of Revelation is ultimately not a book of terror but a book of blessing, for it is the assurance that no matter how much injustice may prevail, no matter how much sin may increase, there will come a time when God establishes true justice and brings judgment upon wickedness. While it may seem that sin and evil are winning the day, God, in His righteous wrath, will bring an end to the prevalence of corruption that began in the garden of Eden. It was this message that gave Henry Wadsworth Longfellow hope in the dark days of the Civil War when he penned the refrain, "God is not dead, nor doth he sleep; the wrong shall fail, the right prevail, with peace on earth, good-will to men" ("I Heard the Bells on Christmas Day")[18]. As the world continues to descend into moral chaos and lawlessness, our hope is not found in politicians or movements but in a God who will execute righteous judgment and bring justice to an unjust world.

---

18. Justin Taylor, "The True Story of Pain and Hope Behind "'I heard the Bells on Christmas Day."'" https://www.thegospelcoalition.org/blogs/justin-taylor/the-story-of-pain-and-hope-behind-i-heard-the-bells-on-christmas-day/ Accessed 9/28/2021

Delighting in God

*Lift up your eyes on high and see who has created
these stars, the One who leads forth out their host by
number, He calls them all by name.*
Isaiah 40:26

In recent years there has been an emphasis on Christianity as a relationship with God rather than a religion. While there are some elements of truth to that, there is also a false dichotomy between the two. When people refer to Christianity as a relationship rather than a religion, they often attempt to divorce Christianity from a set of rules and regulations. However, by necessity, faith involves doctrines, practices, beliefs, attitudes, actions, and a relationship that is driven by the teaching of Scripture, which results in a life of obedience. Yet, just as there is a false religion (i.e., religious practices contrary to Scripture or that distort Scripture), there is also a wrong relationship with God. A false relationship is focused upon the pursuit of personal happiness rather than a relationship with God that results in obedience to His Word. In an inappropriate relationship, we compartmentalize our faith rather than integrating our faith into all aspects of life.

Just as our doctrines, practices, and beliefs are only authentic when they adhere to the teachings and principles of the Bible, so our relationship with God is genuine only when it is driven by the desire to know God and become like Him in every thought, attitude, and action. This is what brings us to our delight in God. David understood what it meant to have an authentic relationship with God. In 1 Samuel 13:14, we find that David was a man who was after God's own heart. This may seem like a strange affirmation, for David's life was marred by sin and failure. We find that David committed adultery, told lies, and committed murder. In addition, he failed as a father, resulting in a highly dysfunctional family. So why did God consider David a man after His own heart even though he was flawed and frequently failed to be obedient?

The answer lies in Psalm 37:3–4. David begins the psalm with a warning about being envious of the wicked. At first glance, the lives of the wicked seem to indicate that they enjoy prosperity despite their evil. However, instead of being envious, David calls upon us to trust in God and find our delight in Him (v. 4). This verse has often been misquoted to suggest that God gives us whatever we desire if we have enough faith. But this is not a blank check for prayer. Instead, it is a redirection of the focus of our prayer. The first line illustrates this principle when David states that we are to delight in God. The point that he is making is not that we are to take pleasure in God because He has blessed us, but that we are to delight in Him and Him alone.

In contrast to the wicked, who find their delight in material possessions, our joy is to be found in the person of God. He becomes the object of our desire. When we delight in God, He becomes the yearning of our soul. The Westminster Shorter Catechism captured this: the question it asks is, "What is the chief end of man?" The answer is then given: "Man's chief end is to glorify God and to enjoy him forever."

This changes everything. Instead of pursuing our own pleasures and desires, we become consumed with the pursuit of God. Instead of being preoccupied with our happiness, we become preoccupied with knowing God and finding our fulfillment in

Him. He becomes the source of our happiness and joy. When we are struggling with adversity, it is easy to become focused on the present circumstances. We become obsessed with finding relief. However, in our pursuit of freedom from trouble, we often sacrifice the significant to obtain the insignificant. We disregard the eternal in our quest to be satisfied only with the temporal. We miss our salvation's real purpose when we only desire to attain freedom from the past and its destructive consequence in our lives. Eternal life is found in the pursuit of God. Christ points this out in John 17:3 when He states, "This is eternal life, that they may know You, the only true God, and Jesus Christ whom You have sent." The purpose of our salvation is to save us from sin so that we will find our complete delight in God. The purpose of this journey in the study of God's attributes was not to know about God, nor was it to provide us the avenue to be free from life's trials; instead, it was to change our whole outlook on life. When God is our delight, it no longer matters what circumstances we face. We study the attributes of God so that we might have a greater insight into God and revel in the totality of His being. Then we can learn to rejoice in every circumstance.

Day 1
Delighting in God: Knowing Him, Not Just Knowing About Him

Read Philippians 3:7–16

That I may know Him and the power of His resurrection. Philippians 3:10

It is one thing to know about someone; it is quite another to have an in-depth personal relationship grounded in mutual understanding. It is easy to reduce God to a series of character qualities that we define and compartmentalize in our quest to "know God." While it is helpful to examine (as we have done) the different attributes that Scripture highlights to help us gain a fuller understanding of who God is, the danger is that we view God solely from a theological and academic perspective. Yet, God is a person. Consequently, to honestly know God, we must move beyond just knowing about God; we must pursue a knowledge of God grounded in an ongoing personal relationship. We can read a book that serves to describe a historical figure to learn about the individual. Yet, this is vastly different from our intimate knowledge of our spouse gleaned after spending years together observing and interacting with them on a daily basis. Because we relate to our spouses through our everyday experience, our knowledge of them as people is ever-growing and expanding. Each day, we discover new nuances and insights into how they think, react, and feel.

For Paul, God is a person, so our knowledge of Him must be grounded in a personal, growing relationship, not just a series of statements gathered from the study of a theological book. In the Greek language, there are two words for "know." The first word, *oida*, is used primarily to refer to cognitive knowledge. The second word, and the one used in our passage, is *ginosko*, which means knowing someone or something experientially; that is, knowledge gained from personal experience. While studying God's attributes can give us a cognitive understanding of who God is, it can be academic and detached. However, Paul desires a far more in-depth knowledge, a knowledge grounded in a personal relationship that unites us with Christ so that we share in His being and His experiences. It is this knowledge that is continually growing and requires constant nurturing, development, and cultivation. It is profoundly personal and individual.

The tragedy is that too many Christians just know about God, but few truly know God. Paul made this his aim in life; it was so valuable to Paul that everything else paled in comparison. Paul would gladly give up every achievement, every possession, every honor, every dream to grow in his relationship with Christ. There was no cost too great for Paul in his quest to know Christ and become like Christ by sharing in Christ's suffering and righteousness.

Understanding of my wife can only come through years of personal interaction with her. It requires making it my priority to daily gain a greater understanding of her as a person. So, it is also true that my relationship with Christ can only be developed through daily interaction. To know Christ, I must cultivate my relationship with Him through prayer, the study of His Word, and allowing Him to reveal Himself to me amid the struggles and difficulties of life. The term "surpassing value" (Philippians 3:8) refers to that which is of such exceptional value that there is nothing comparable. So today, ask Christ to make Himself real to you, not just as a theological truth, but as a person who desires to share Himself with you so that you might become like Him. God wants a personal relationship with you, grounded in His self-revelation in Scripture but developed through personal interaction in daily life.

Day 2
Delighting in God: Thirsting for God

Read Psalm 63:1–11

My soul thirsts for You; my flesh yearns for You.
Psalm 63:1

In the region of southern Israel, the land is a barren, hot desert where little grows. It is a wilderness where water is scarce, and there is little shade to protect one from the scorching sun that beats down upon anyone who travels there. It is a place where thirst would be one's constant companion, and water would be one's obsession. Into this wasteland David was forced to flee when his son, Absalom, sought to usurp the throne and wrest the kingdom away from him (2 Samuel 15–18). However, David did not just discover the barren wilderness of southern Judah as he found himself fleeing for refuge; he also experienced the wasteland of his soul. One can only imagine the despair David must have felt as he found himself sitting under the hot Judean sun. His son had betrayed him and turned against him. We see the depth of David's pain when he lamented Absalom's death: "O my son Absalom, my son, my son Absalom! Would I had died instead of you, O Absalom, my son, my son" (2 Samuel 18:33).

In this wilderness, both literal and figurative, David penned the words of Psalm 63. When one reads the psalm, one can easily hear the echo of David's circumstances as his words speak of thirst "in a dry and weary land where there is no water" (v. 1). Surprisingly, the psalm is not a psalm of lament, in which the writer would cry in deep grief because of his circumstances. It is not a psalm in which David prays for God's deliverance and the restoration of his throne. Instead, in this psalm we find David in deep longing, not for a change in his circumstances, but for God Himself. During one of the darkest periods of his life, what David longed for most was a fresh vision of God. David was not just facing physical thirst; he was confronted with spiritual thirst.

If you have ever been thirsty, you know that water becomes your one thought. The drier your mouth becomes, the more you think only of a cool, refreshing drink of water. In his longing and thirst in his wilderness experience, David's one thought was of being satisfied by the power and glory of God. So powerful was David's longing for God that it became his one thought day and night. When sleep escaped him because he had to remain watchful for his enemies, he thought only of God (v. 6). In verse 8, he states that he will cling to God. The word *cling* speaks of a deep, unbreakable attachment. The term can be translated "to be glued" or "joined fast with another." For David, his one longing was to remain riveted upon God.

This is what we have lost in our modern Christianity. God is no longer our longing. To satisfy the cravings of our soul, we turn to all other activities rather than God. We strive for theological integrity, and rightfully so. Yet, we have forgotten that the endgame is not theological correctness but a personal relationship with the living God. We no longer thirst for God. We no longer find our satisfaction in God Himself (v. 5). How do we change? It begins by developing a thirst for God and not being satisfied until we find Him. Second, we need to cultivate a desire to have a personal relationship—so much so that it becomes our constant prayer and thought. This begins by asking God to give us what is not natural for sinful man: a longing for Him. This is a prayer that God promises to answer. In the Sermon on the Mount, Christ stated, "Blessed are those who hunger and thirst for righteousness, for they shall be satisfied" (Matthew 5:6). Today, start to make it your daily prayer that God will give you a longing for Him.

Day 3
Delighting in God: Finding Our Delight in God

Read Psalm 37

Delight yourself in the LORD and He will give you the desires of your heart. Psalm 37:4

What do you delight in? What gives you pleasure and joy in life? Indeed, we find delight and joy in circumstances and events. We find joy in seeing a brilliantly colored sunrise or sunset. We enjoy a sense of pleasure when we accomplish a meaningful task. We enjoy time spent working on a hobby. While we find delight in events, our greatest joys and pleasures come in connection with the people we care about. While enjoying the beautiful sunset, we experience greater pleasure when sharing it with someone we love. We may enjoy the beauty of a sunset for a moment, but when we share it with another, it becomes a lasting and cherished memory.

Psalm 37 is an alphabetic psalm, in which each subsequent thought is introduced by the following letter in the Hebrew alphabet. The psalmist begins with a sense of urgency, frontloading the psalm with imperatives. While there are seventeen imperatives (or direct commands) interwoven in the psalm, eleven of them are found in verses 3–8. In these verses, we are commanded to "trust in the LORD, do good; dwell in the land, cultivate faithfulness; delight yourself in the Lord . . . Commit your ways to the LORD, trust also in Him . . . Rest in the LORD, wait patiently for Him . . . Cease from anger, and forsake wrath." While it is easy to become envious of those who seem to enjoy success in life as they live without consideration of God, the psalmist wants us to have a different focus. Instead of delighting in the pursuits of prosperity and success by the world's standard, we are to center our lives on our relationship with God. We are to find our delight in God.

The word "delight" has the sense of having a high degree of pleasure or mental satisfaction in something. The mark of the wicked is that they find their delight in the pleasures of this world. For them, the pursuit of a relationship with God is meaningless and dull. This is not the case for those who desire to know God. When God becomes our delight, then everything else diminishes in comparison. To understand what it means to delight in the Lord, we must realize that it is an outgrowth of the commands He has given in verse 3. Satisfaction comes when we fully trust in the Lord and make it our goal to do what is right. When we do so, then God gives us the desires of our hearts. However, the order here is crucial. We do not delight in God because He has given us our desires, but instead, we rejoice in God when we bring our deepest longings to God so that we find them fulfilled in Him. When we make God our yearning and delight, we find that it is in our relationship with Him that our desires are fully realized. This stands in contrast to the world, which places its desire on the pursuit of material prosperity and success. In the end, instead of fulfilling their longings, people of the world find that they are devoid of them (vv. 35–36).

Delighting in God realigns your whole perspective of life. Seek Him and make Him the object of your longings. This means that the pursuit of your relationship with him becomes your highest priority. Here lies the question: do you delight in God so that He becomes your priority? Do you find your joy in Him? Do the church and the worship of God take precedence over all other activities or are they secondary in importance? Would you rather spend your day pursuing an endeavor or spend it in the study of His Word?

Day 4
Delighting in God Through Prayer

Read Philippians 4:4–7; James 4:1–4; Hebrew 4:14–16

Be anxious for nothing, but in everything by prayer . . . let your requests be made know to God.
Philippians 4:6

Of all the religious activities we do, prayer is often the most frequent but the least understood. This is because we approach prayer like Aladdin viewed the genie. For Aladdin, the genie was there to grant his wishes and solve all his problems. In the same way, we view prayer as the means of enticing God to do what we desire.

Of all the demonstrations of God's grace in our salvation and daily life, perhaps there is none more remarkable than the invitation to pray. It is not just that God allows us the privilege to pray, but that he *commands* us to pray and to come with boldness into His presence. For the Old Testament saints, the idea of seeking a personal audience with God was unthinkable. God could only be approached by the priests, and even then with much caution and preparation. All this changed when Christ became the final substitutionary sacrifice. Through His death, we now have complete and continual access to God. The word that the writer uses in Hebrews 4:16 refers to the attitude of being willing to do that which involves risk or danger, like a firefighter who boldly rushes into a burning house to save a family. So, we are invited to be bold in our approach with God because Christ has removed the risk of judgment.

Not only are we to pray with boldness, but we are also to pray about everything. God invites us to share every issue in life with Him, especially those causing us anxiety and concern. Then, not only can we pray with confidence, but we can pray with thanksgiving because we are assured of His response. The result is that we can have peace, knowing that He will act on our behalf and provide the answer we are desperately seeking.

Now we come to the heart of prayer. We do not see answers to prayer not because we do not pray but because we ask with the wrong motives and attitudes. When we pray, we often do so with the desire for God to conform His actions to our will. We pray to obtain God's approval and blessings for the plans we make. Yet this fails to understand the purpose of prayer. We are to pray, not to bend God's will to our desires, but to adjust our desires and will to His. In teaching us to pray, Christ begins with the request, "Your will be done on earth as it is in heaven" (Matthew 6:10). When we face issues in life, instead of asking God to do what we desire, our request should be that His will would be accomplished in and through us amid the circumstances we face. Thus, effective prayer begins with a prayer of submission rather than a request for our desires and wishes to be met. This is the type of prayer that Paul refers to when He states that we are to pray continually (1 Thessalonians 5:17).

Make it your goal to be more prayerful in all your activities, not just asking God to do what you desire, but asking God to fulfill His desire in you. So, for example, as you encounter difficulties and challenges, instead of just asking God to eliminate the trials you face (which is undoubtedly an appropriate request), also ask that God will enable you to accomplish His will amid these circumstances. Then your prayer will be powerful, for that is the prayer God delights to answer. Then you can rest in peace, knowing that His will is always perfect and good.

Day 5
Delighting in God: Becoming Thankful

Read Psalm 13

I will sing to the Lord *because he has dealt bountifully with me.* Psalm 13:6

Amid adversity, it is easy to complain. When facing ongoing challenges, we focus on our problems and start to grumble about what God has done. The hymnwriter Charles Wesley wrote, "O for a thousand tongues to sing our great Redeemer's praise," yet it is much easier to use our one tongue to sing our complaints about life.

At first glance at Psalm 13, it seems as if David is singing a song of protest. Known as one of the "lament psalms," the song gives voice to the struggles and trials David was facing. This was no mere bad day; David faced ongoing challenges and enemies that threatened his very life. All this led to a crisis of his faith. When he needed God's protective intervention, God was hiding from him. Instead of God's promises being a source of comfort, they became a source of mockery. For example, in Deuteronomy 4:31, God promises that He would not forget the covenant He made with His people; however, David felt God had forgotten him!

Just when it seems that David will fall into a pit of despair and lose all faith in God's salvation, the song takes a sudden turn. The abrupt change in the tone of the psalm between verses 4 and 5 is jolting in its dramatic difference. Having become convinced that his enemies will triumph over him because of God's neglect, David suddenly reaffirms his trust in the faithful love of God. Just when he is on the brink of complete hopelessness and his heart seems to be enveloped in sorrow (v. 2), his heart unexpectedly rejoices, and he sings a song of praise and joy (v. 5). What changed? There is nothing in the text that would indicate that his circumstances changed. What changed was his focus. Instead of dwelling on his misery and adversaries, he riveted his thinking onto the love of God. He was reminded of how God had dwelt bountifully with him (v. 6), that God had done abundant good on his behalf.

Our joy in life is not determined by our circumstances but by our perspective. We can either become focused on our problems and hardships or remain focused on God's blessing and goodness. We change our focus when we start to sing the praises of

God and start being thankful for all that He has done for us. This is what Paul focuses upon in Philippians 4:6. We often focus on the first part of the verse in which he commands us to pray rather than be anxious. Yet, we often neglect the second part of the verse, which provides the key to changing our outlook—that is, to integrate thanksgiving into our prayers. While prayer reminds us of our dependency upon God, thanksgiving reminds us of what God has done and will do. It shifts our focus from the problems we face to the God who sustains us.

With all the challenges in our lives, we can quickly become discouraged and pessimistic. Both David and Paul remind us to be thankful by focusing on who God is and what He has done. Spend more time being grateful for what God has done rather than grumbling about the circumstances around you. Then your perspective will change, and you will discover genuine joy, even if the situation around you remains the same.

Seeking God

How blessed are those who observe his testimonies,
who seek him with all their heart.
Psalm 119:2

To be a follower of Christ and one who delights in God requires that we make God the object of our affections and the focus of our lives. In our Christian lives, we have become dependent upon others and the church for our spiritual growth. While the church is central to God's redemptive program and His purpose for our lives, we must accept responsibility for our spiritual development. What we desire and seek is what we attain and become.

As we saw at the beginning of this journey, this is the starting point of our search to know God, and it is also the ending point of the expedition. Throughout Scripture, we are commanded to seek God. In Psalm 14:2, we find that "the LORD looked down from heaven upon the sons of men to see if there are any who understand, who seek after God." To seek the Lord is to investigate Him diligently. One of the great blessings that God has given us is the invitation to search Him out, to become a student of Him. God desires us to know Him and to delve into the depth of His character. This is the self-disclosure of God. From the first day of God's creative event, He sought to reveal Himself to us.

First, He imprinted His being within creation itself. Like a craftsman who uses his craftmanship to reveal his character, God intertwined His nature within His handiwork so that we might see Him. Paul writes in Romans 1:20, "For since the creation of the world His invisible attributes, that is, His eternal power and divine nature, have been perceived, being understood through what has been made, so that they are without excuse." The study of creation was meant to be the study of God. Every science, every study that delves into the secrets of the laws of nature, should ultimately end in the proclamation and discovery of God. The scientist is foremost a theologian who exegetes creation to discover the being of God. This is the most incredible privilege afforded to man. We were created in His image to learn and explore His being. When we look upon creation, we should see more than a beautiful picture—we should see God Himself.

Second, not only did God reveal Himself in creation; He then wrote His autobiography, His love letter to us to give us a greater understanding of who He is and what He desires. Thus, the Bible is not just a book about living before God; it is a book on God Himself. It is His self-disclosure to us. In God's Word and all His commands, He set forth to make Himself known to us so that we "may become partakers of the divine nature" (2 Peter 1:4). Thus, in every word, every page, every event recorded in the pages of the Bible, we find the self-disclosure of God.

Then God did the unthinkable. In the great act of love, God came to earth to walk among us. No longer was He a God who resided in heaven, or even a God who describes Himself in the written word; He was a God who dwelt among us that we might know Him personally and intimately. Jesus walked with the disciples to reveal the Father in all His glory and nature. He was Emmanuel—God with us.

This brings us to our greatest goal, and that is to seek Him. The psalmist captures the importance of seeking God when he writes in Psalm 63:1, "O God, You are my God; I shall seek You earnestly; My soul thirsts for You, my flesh yearns for You, in a dry and weary land where there is no water." Just as the body craves water, so our soul longs for God, to know Him.

This is what brings us to the heart of being a disciple of Christ. The word *disciple* means a learner—but a learner of what? We often think that being a disciple is learning about the Christian faith and the Christian life. However, that misses the point: a disciple is dedicated to learning about God. Therefore, we set our minds on things above (Colossians 3:2), not because of the wonders of heaven, but because of the wonders of God.

When we are going through trials, the greatest tragedy is when we lose sight of God. Our quest to know God becomes replaced with the search for a life free from struggles. When that happens, we miss the joy of knowing God, for not only has God revealed Himself in creation, in His Word, and in the life of Christ, He also reveals himself through our suffering. Job's most meaningful lesson in his suffering was not Why, but Who. God did not reveal the answer to Job's questions regarding suffering; instead, He manifested Himself. In the end, that is all we need to know.

Day 1
Seeking God: Setting the Right Priority in Life

Luke 10:38–42

But only one thing is necessary. Luke 10:42

In 1984 Charles Hummel wrote a bestseller entitled *Tyranny of the Urgent*. Today we would have to write a companion book entitled *Tyranny of the Insignificant*. We hit the ground running in the morning and go non-stop until our heads hit the pillow at night. But what do we strive to attain?

In this passage in Luke, we find a snapshot of the daily life of a family. Mary and Martha were close friends with Jesus and maintained a special relationship with Him. In John 11:5, John writes, "Now Jesus loved Martha and her sister and Lazarus," so it was natural that Jesus would be staying at their home. Furthermore, because demonstrating hospitality was paramount within their culture, it is not astonishing when Martha becomes overwhelmed in preparing a meal for Jesus (and presumably the disciples as well). The failure to do so would have been a profound embarrassment and cultural faux pas. What is surprising is Mary's unwillingness to help. Instead, she remained seated at Jesus's feet, listening to His conversation. While Martha was caught up in caring for the physical needs, Mary focused on the spiritual. At first glance, we would naturally side with Martha. While she is working diligently to provide for her guests, Mary is sitting—activities of the urgent versus quiet repose and idleness. When Martha's patience runs out, she elicits Jesus's help in getting Mary to fulfill her responsibilities. Surprisingly, Jesus does not rebuke Mary (who placed the spiritual need above cultural expectation) but instead rebukes Martha (who was driven by cultural expectations rather than the spiritual opportunity to listen to Jesus teach). When Christ states, "Only one thing is necessary," He is not referring to a simple meal's adequacy. The one thing He is referring to is the His teaching. Christ realigns Martha's perspective by redirecting Her attention from the physical—the temporary and the insignificant—to the spiritual, the eternal, and the important. He is reminding her that "man shall not live by bread alone, but on every word that proceeds out of the mouth of God" (Matthew 4:4).

This is the tragedy of our day: the tyranny of the insignificant clouds our concept of what is truly important. Too often, we are Martha. We fill our days with activities and no longer have time for what is eternally significant. We are just plain too busy, but the things occupying our minds and demanding our time are unimportant and have no lasting benefit or consequence. We spend our days working harder to make more money to buy more things to fill bigger houses, but, in the end, these become nothing more than fodder for the garbage heap. The truly eternal things are pushed aside by the obsession with the present. We are too busy to read our Bibles, go to church, or build relationships with people that have an eternal impact. We become like Martha. To pursue a relationship with God requires us to rearrange our time and energies. We do not need more time in our day; we need to rearrange our whole focus to a point where our pursuit of Christ becomes our chief goal, where time spent with Him is the highest priority in our lives. At the end of life, there is still only one crucial thing, and that is what Mary chose. What is it that you have chosen?

Day 2
Seeking God: Finding Perspective in Life

Read: Psalm 27:1–14

One thing I have asked from the LORD, that I shall seek: that I may dwell in the house of the LORD all the days of my life. Psalm 27:4

What is our prayer when we are facing struggles and adversity? David could fully relate to the turmoil that comes when life seems to press in around us. We see in this psalm hints of the deep valleys of life he has traversed. David faced times when people unjustly sought his life, when armies relentlessly pursued him with the sole purpose of killing him (vv. 3, 6; 1 Samuel 21–23). He faced rejection by his own family when they turned against him (Psalm 27:10; 2 Samuel 15). He knew the pain of God's heavy hand of discipline when the guilt of his sin was overwhelming (Psalm 27:9; 2 Samuel 11). David had experienced times when those closest to him turned against him and betrayed him with false accusations (Psalm 27:12; 2 Samuel 15:31). Yet, what gave him confidence and hope throughout these experiences was his trust in God. Even with all of David's spiritual and moral failures, why did God affirm that David was a man after His own heart (1 Samuel 13:14)? How could David have such peace in the face of such overwhelming circumstances? The answer lies in David's focus.

In these verses, we see the focus of David that distinguished him from others. What David desired more than anything was to be "in the house of the LORD all the days of my life to behold the beauty of the LORD and to meditate in His temple" (Psalm 27:4). His prayer was not that God would deliver him from all of his problems, but that God would allow him to spend his life in the temple, engaged in the worship of God.

For David, the worship of and meditation on Scripture was his greatest delight and desire. For him, the greatest joy was to spend the day at the temple just reflecting on the intrinsic beauty of God's nature and character. This is what distinguishes him from the rest. In our prayers, is our focus on what we want God to do for us or on how we want God to reveal Himself to us? To behold the beauty of the Lord captures the essence of worship. It is what brings perspective to life. Beholding the beauty of the Lord begins with contemplating and enjoying the character and attributes of God. We discover our delight when we reflect upon his character and upon all the good things He has done for us. This brings us back to our focus in life. When we focus upon the problems and struggles of life, the result is discouragement. When our focus is on our circumstances, our problems become over-whelming. Therefore, David redirects his focus to God. Because God is his delight, and he meditates on the wonders of God's activities, all the problems and troubles he faced in life become inconsequential.

Today, direct your mind to contemplate the wonder and joy of God rather than to dwell on the news and problems of the day. When your God becomes big, your problems become small. As God reveals Himself to you through His Word, look for His activity in your daily life. Make it your daily prayer to seek the delights of God's character, for that is a prayer that God desires in us (v. 8).

Day 3
Seeking God When Life is Barren

Deuteronomy 4:25–31

Seek the LORD *your God, and you will find Him.*
Deuteronomy 4:29

Deuteronomy is Moses's final message to the people of Israel before he passes the leadership baton to Joshua and rides off into the sunset. The message he gave was proclaimed on the east side of the Jordan River just before the Israelites crossed over to take possession of the land promised to Abraham. He delivers his message that day to the second generation of those who came out of the land of Egypt. Because of their disobedience, the first generation (all those over twenty years of age who had come out of Egypt) had died wandering in the wilderness. So, on this day,

Moses reaffirms the covenant God had made with the nation at Mt. Sinai.

Even as he reaffirms the covenant with the new generation, he also gives a solemn warning that their future will not always be rosy. Moses understood the human sin nature. Even though spirits were high and the people had affirmed their loyalty to God, he knows that people are fickle and that they, like their fathers, will also rebel against God. It will not be long before they adapt to the culture and religious practices of their surroundings (v. 25). As a result, just as their fathers and mothers experienced God's discipline, so will God again discipline the people of Israel. Instead of enjoying all the blessings God has promised, they will face the certainty of His judgment and will be scattered in foreign countries. His words would quickly be realized during the time of the Judges, when Israel would go through a series of cycles of prosperity, idolatry, judgment, conquest, repentance, and then deliverance.

However, even as Moses warns the people of their future failure and judgment, he gives them an incredible promise of hope. Even after they have rebelled, if they seek God, God promise that He will restore them, for He is a compassionate God. The picture of God's compassion is of a father who looks intently and lovingly upon his children; in the same way, God will continually show mercy and grace even when His people rebel against Him. Instead of destroying them, He will stay faithful to His promises even when the people have proven to be unfaithful.

In these times of spiritual and emotional emptiness, we find the fresh hope of God's promises. If we are willing to renew our search for Him, He will reveal himself to us. However, this search must involve complete surrender to Him. To search for Him with your heart and soul implies that He becomes the focus of your longing. Thus, the word *return* in verse 30 is also translated as "to repent." It means to turn away from the pursuit of our will and surrender to His.

Even if your life seems filled with distress and despair, and God seems absent and heaven silent, there is hope, and that hope is found in seeking Him with your whole heart. So today, ask God to reveal Himself to you in a fresh and new way and then pursue Him in the pages of Scripture, and you will find that He will reveal Himself to you.

Day 4
Seeking God: Realigning Our Focus

Read Luke 12:22–32

Do not worry about your life ... but seek His kingdom, and these things will be added to you. Luke 12:22,31

Uncertainty breeds fear and worry. As we listen to the news today, it seems that life is continually thrown into confusion and apprehension. The political landscape is in turmoil as political ideologies clash. Once aligned to a Judeo-Christian ethic, the moral compass of our nation is spinning wildly in search of some moral direction. No longer is there a sense of absolute truth, but instead, our morality is dictated by personal relativity. *I* determine what is right and wrong. Secularism, which defines morality apart from any consideration of God, is now driving the moral compass, and the new morality strives to silence anyone who disagrees. Under the guise of pluralism and inclusion, they run roughshod over any voice of dissent. No longer is biblical truth admired; it is now seen as a threat. All of this leads to apprehension and anxiety about the future.

However, Christ breaks through the fog of our anxiety and realigns our perspective. In many ways, we have adapted to the culture around us where success, financial security, and the pursuit of personal happiness without moral restraint are desired. Today we have become entrapped by the tyranny of the insignificant. The things we think are essential—having adequate food, appropriate clothing, and proper housing—are, in the end, non-essential, yet these are the things that dictate our thoughts. Consequently, when we are truly honest with ourselves, all the things that we become so focused on are ultimately temporary and, in light of eternity, insignificant. This is not to say that it is wrong to enjoy the material blessings that God has given us, but rather that we should never make these things the goal and purpose of our lives.

Instead of becoming focused on the accumulation of stuff or the pursuit of the temporary, we are to focus on the eternal, and the only lasting thing is the kingdom of God. What then does this mean? How do we seek His kingdom? The kingdom of God is the advancement of His rule in our lives and the world. To seek the kingdom of God is to seek to obtain and reveal His righteousness in our lives. It is to proclaim the gospel so that people are freed from the bondage of their sinful desires and find true liberty in the joy of a relationship with God. The arrival of His kingdom is our longing and our hope. It is to be at the heartbeat of our prayer. It is what Christ points us to when, in the Lord's Prayer, He teaches us to pray, "Your Kingdom come, Your will be done on earth as it is in Heaven." This is not an elusive pursuit, where we hope to attain the impossible. Instead, Christ promises that the Father will gladly give us His kingdom when we make it our desire (Luke 12:32).

Our pursuit of God is what grounds our hope in the person of Christ. He has given us the promise that when our focus is on Him and the attainment of His kingdom, then He will take care of us and provide for all we need. Because He has promised us the lesser (our daily food and clothing), we are free to pursue the greater: participation in the kingdom of God. Because He will establish his kingdom, we no longer need to worry about the events of the day, for the uncertainty of today is never a threat to the certainty of His kingdom. Where is your focus today?

Day 5
Seeking God: Finding Contentment in All Circumstances

Read 2 Corinthians 12:1–10

My grace is sufficient for you . . . therefore I am well content with weaknesses . . . 2 Corinthians 12:9

When we think of contentment, we often focus on our attitudes toward money and possessions. But genuine fulfillment goes far beyond these. Learning to be content requires that we discover joy in all circumstances. It is one thing to be satisfied with our financial portfolio; it is quite another to be content with every situation and status in life. In 2 Corinthians 12, Paul recounts the incredible experience he had when he was allowed a privilege very few humans have experienced, the opportunity to have a glimpse of heaven. Such an experience could easily result in pride and a feeling of spiritual superiority. To prevent Paul from becoming spiritually arrogant, God brought adversity into his life. Biblical commentators have widely speculated concerning the proverbial "thorn in the flesh." Some suggest that it was some form of spiritual hardship, such as demonic oppression. Others hypothesize it was a struggle with a particular temptation or his profound guilt and remorse for his violence against the church. It may have involved physical difficulties such as periodic bouts of malaria or the frustration of being nearly blind because of eye damage suffered from his persecution and beatings or disease affecting his eyesight. Finally, some commentators have suggested emotional struggles stemming from depression or the ongoing effects of stress in his ministry. Each has some biblical support from the writings of Paul. Whatever the circumstance, it was sufficiently troubling to Paul that he earnestly prayed for God to bring him relief.

Surprisingly, God does not answer Paul's request by bringing deliverance from the situation weighing heavily upon him. Instead, God reminded Paul of His sufficient grace. Paul needed to realize that his contentment in life comes from God's grace rather than his circumstances. Serenity is more than just being content with God's provision for our physical and material needs. Contentment also encompasses our attitude in the face of life's daily challenges. Sometimes it is easier to be content when we have our daily needs met, but it can be challenging to be satisfied in adverse circumstances. Yet, this is what Paul learned. Because of his awareness of God's grace, which brought assurance of his salvation and eternal standing before God, he could be content in every condition of life, no matter what it might be. Thus, Paul could be grateful in the face of persecution and attacks. He could be satisfied with his shortcomings and weaknesses. He could be content when life seemed overwhelming.

Paul brings us back again to the work of God's grace. Paul could be content in every circumstance because he saw all things that happened in his life as the work of God, not only to develop his character but also to minister more effectively to others. It taught him that our sufficiency comes from God rather than from ourselves. Therefore, he would boast about his weaknesses. While we tend to operate from the platform of our skills and strengths, Paul recognizes that real power comes when we function from the platform of our weaknesses and imperfections. It was in his weakness that God's power became most evident. The awareness of God's empowerment in our weaknesses becomes the springboard for inward contentment. Contentment comes when we realize that God uses all circumstances and situations to achieve His purpose for His glory, and there is no greater joy than this. Serenity comes when God becomes our focus instead of our circumstances; when we seek Him rather than pleasure and comfort. Are we content to allow God to bring adversity into our lives so that He might be glorified?

Discovering Joy Through the Worship of God

You alone are the LORD. You have made the heavens, the heaven of heavens with all their host, the earth and all that is on it, the seas and all that is in them. You gave life to all of them, and the heavenly hosts bow down before You.

Nehemiah 9:6

All the paths of the Christian life lead ultimately to the expression of worship, including the way of suffering. Woven through the pages of Scripture is the call to worship God and to exalt Him. It is the goal of our creation and the focus of God's angelic beings. When we worship, we join the activities of angels, and we enter the very throne room of heaven.

Yet as crucial as worship is, it often becomes misguided. Too often, we measure worship by the experience we have. When we come to a worship service, the focus is often on how it makes us feel. Does it lift us emotionally and give us a sense of God's presence and nearness? Because of the focus on our emotional experience, the worship service becomes more of a performance designed to elicit an emotional response than an acknowledgment of God. Worship becomes equated with music and the rituals we perform on Sunday. Ultimately, the focus becomes upon us and some form of spiritual self-gratification. How often have people left a church because the music or the service did not give them the experience they craved? When this happens, worship then becomes more about us and our experience than about God.

But the worship of God is much more, and the focus of reverence is never on what we experience, but rather on God and the praise of Him. In Psalm 148, the writer calls upon us to join the voices of all creation in proclaiming the praises of God by acknowledging His divine nature and His glory above the earth. This is the starting point of worship. Worship begins with the realization that God is infinite and that He cannot be contained in the space of a temple or church; that He is infinitely more significant than the whole universe. Worship begins with realizing His transcendence: that He exists apart from creation and is exalted above all creation. This moves the focus of worship from ourselves to a new emphasis on God. To understand worship is to divest ourselves of focusing on our experience and to direct our focus to God. God, not ourselves, is the object and direction of worship.

The concept of "worship" begins with the proper fear of God. While we often think of the fear of God as a sense of reverence, it should not be entirely divorced from the element of terror. To fear God is to treat Him as holy, to stand in awe of God. It is not to take Him lightly or regard Him with a sense of flippant commonness. It is this fear that then leads to righteous living. Because it motivates us to live righteously, worship is also joined with submission. The basic meaning of the Hebrew word for worship is to bow down and prostrate oneself before another. It is to do homage and surrender to a superior. This is seen in the New Testament, where worship involves both the attitude and the position of bowing down and pledging one's alliance to God. At the core of worship is not our feelings or experience, but our acknowledgment of and submission to God. This is why an unbeliever can't worship, for there is no submission. Too often, we worship God in arrogance rather than humble surrender.

To worship God, then, involves recognizing and responding to who God is and what He has done for us, through our submission and service to Him in all aspects of life. As such, worship involves the following multifaceted response to God:

- *Worship involves an active response.* Worship is not just an internal attitude or a static feeling; it is a lifestyle revealed in our actions toward others and God. It is not passively sitting in a pew watching others perform.
- *Worship is God-centered.* Worship involves recognizing the nature and character of God as He has revealed Himself. To worship God, we must accept Him for who He is and how He has revealed Himself throughout all of Scripture rather than understand Him based on our perspective. Worship lets God be God on His terms.
- *Worship involves a response to God's grace and his works of salvation on our behalf.*
- *Worship involves submission.* It consists of recognizing that we are subject to God's will and purpose.
- *Worship involves service.* To truly worship involves acts of service to build God's kingdom, expressed through our service to His church.
- *Worship encompasses the whole life.* It is not just what happens on Sunday morning during the music; it is to be lived daily, with the focus continually on Him.

This is where all paths in our Christian lives are to lead us. Sometimes the best route is the one through suffering, for, in our grief, we learn to recognize our frailty and weakness. In travail, we are reminded of our finiteness. This leads us to a greater awareness of God's infinite nature and power and glory, which is where we find our ultimate joy.

Day 1
The People God Seeks

Read John 4:7–26

True worshipers will worship the Father in spirit and truth; for such people the Father seeks to be His worshipers. John 4:23

She was an outcast among outcasts. To the Jews, the Samaritans were the lowest of the low. Not only had they conflicted with the Jews politically, but they had distorted the Jewish faith, having their version of the Pentateuch (first five books of the Old Testament) that brought them into religious conflict with the Jews. Consequently, there remained a deep and longstanding hatred between the Jews and the Samaritans driven not just by ethnicity and politics but also by religion. However, this woman, because of her immoral lifestyle, was an outcast even among the Samaritans. Therefore, for Jesus to talk to this woman was scandalous, for she was both a Samaritan and an adulterer.

When Christ met her at the well that day, she was living a life that was broken and in desperate need of redemption. However, what should arrest our attention is the message He conveyed. In answer to her question about the proper location of worship, Christ elevated her focus to the heart of what worship is. Christ distinguishes between those who are genuine followers of God and those who are charlatans by examining their attitude and response in worship. Christ sets the requirement for praise by pointing out that authentic worship must be done in spirit and truth. The first requirement, "to worship God in spirit," is governed by the statement that "God is spirit." The point Christ makes is that God is invisible and not confined to the physical realm. Therefore, to worship Him in spirit requires a supernatural work of the Holy Spirit, who makes it possible for us to know Him. The second requirement of worship is that we must worship God in truth. Worship must be consistent with the truth of God revealed in His Word and in the person of Christ. When John states that Christ is the Word of God in John 1:1, he affirms that Christ is the self-revelation (i.e., the Word of God) of God to us. He became flesh so that we might know Him. Christ is the truth—the complete and faithful revelation of God. To worship God in truth points to the fact that we must worship through the person of Christ and our identification with Him. For Christ, the redemption this woman needed was to be found only by her spiritual transformation, accomplished by Christ.

This story brings us to the core of our response to God. If Christ is how we can relate to God, then worship of God is the necessary outcome. To truly experience the redemptive work of Christ is to be brought into the awareness of God. Christ is the connecting link between God and us, but worship remains the ultimate response. God's purpose for us is not just found in our salvation from hell and its punishment; it is located in the life-long worship of Him.

The absence of genuine worship in our life becomes a tragedy. In our failure to worship genuinely and continually, we miss out on God's purpose for us. If we are to thrive during the challenges of our day, we can only do so when worship becomes the continual expression of our hearts. The more we worship God, the more we discover what it means to have a relationship with Him.

If you want to experience the full enjoyment of God, learn to worship Him. Make worship central to your life, for that is God's will for you.

Day 2
The Sacrifice of Praise

Read Hebrews 13:7–16

Let us continually offer up a sacrifice of praise to God. Hebrews 13:15

The writer of Hebrews continually reminds us that Christ came to fulfill the law by providing the final sacrifice for our sins. He repeatedly points us back to life under the Old Covenant with its sacrificial system to illustrate the work of Christ on the cross. The Day of Atonement in the Old Testament, with the blood of the sacrifice being sprinkled on the altar in the holy of holies, serves to foreshadow the redemptive purpose of Christ's death. Yet, the foreshadowing is only that: it is a picture until the full reality comes. While the Old Testament sacrifices had to be repeated year after year, Christ's sacrifice for sin was final and complete. In the Old Testament, the people would identify with the offering, and in so doing, their sins were covered by the blood of the sacrifice. However, Christ cleansed us from the stain of our sin by sacrificing His blood, so we gladly bear the reproach and persecution that comes because of it.

If Christ was the final sacrifice for our sins, what is to be our sacrifice? For the writer of Hebrews, the appropriate response to what Christ has done for us is to continually offer up a sacrifice of praise to God, giving thanks to Him for what He has done. This begins with our conversations with others. Praise is not done in the prayer closet but in the open, where we tell others about God and His activity on our behalf. Our adoration of God is public and is shown when we publicly acknowledge God's character to encourage others in the church (Hebrews 10:24–25) and when we confess our faith in Christ before unbelievers. But it is not revealed in word alone; it is also shown in our actions. Thus, the writer goes on to mention doing good and sharing with others. We express our gratitude to God by caring for those in the church facing the adversity of persecution or trials. It is to be concerned about the welfare of others, both for their physical and spiritual needs.

For those who have experienced the salvation of Christ, the praise of God should be natural and ongoing. The original writing of Hebrews 13:15 is even more emphatic. It says, "Through Him, therefore, let us present as an act of worship a sacrifice of praise to God through all things." This makes praise not just continual but all-encompassing. It is to encompass all times and all circumstances.

It is easy to grumble and complain about the trials we face in times of difficulty and hardship. As we go through life, praise becomes spotty at best. Sometimes, when something outstanding happens, we may offer a prayer of thanksgiving, but it hardly flows continually from our lips. Yet this is what the writer is calling us to do. We are to live with the constant affirmation of God's goodness toward us at every point in life, in every situation. We are to reorient our perspective to see the surpassing greatness of our salvation as a reason to praise regardless of what we face in life, both good and bad.

Day 3
Worship: A Glimpse into Heaven

Read Revelation 4:1–11

The twenty-four elders will fall down before Him
who sits on the throne and will worship Him who
lives forever and ever. Revelation 4:10

Revelation is hardly a book we would think about when we think of worship. When someone mentions the book of Revelation, our thoughts go to judgment, plagues, and the final destruction of Satan and his followers. We may think of many things, but worship and praise are hardly among them. When someone mentions worship, our thoughts turn to the Psalms and the songs of praise that are offered on the psalmist's lips. However, when we look closer, we find that the central theme of the book of Revelation is worship. Over half of the New Testament references to the word *worship* are found in the book of Revelation. The book begins with a declaration of worship (Revelation 1:4–8) and ends with a call to worship God alone (Revelation 22:9). Before the outpouring of judgment, there is first the description of the heavens worshiping God (Revelation 5:8–14). After God's judgment, the heavens sing the anthem of praise to the God who executes His justice upon the world (Revelation 19:1–6).

Amid the praise of God's terrifying judgment on the earth, we also find ourselves transported to the wonder of heaven. In a rare glimpse, we are given the privilege of hearing and seeing the constant theme of heaven: the praise of the glory of God. The words we find in Revelation 4:8 echo the same anthem that Isaiah recorded in Isaiah 6. Day and night, the angelic beings encircle the throne, singing the praises of God. Their worship was not just in their pronouncement of praise but also in their submission to Him who sits upon the throne. In verse 10, we find that the twenty-four elders, who are angelic beings given unique authority in heaven, casting down their crowns before God as an act of worship and acknowledgment of God's unparalleled supremacy. Then, in a thunderous anthem of praise, all the angels, beyond human ability to number, join in singing the praises of God. The sound must have been deafening as the halls of heaven reverberated with the confession of God's infinite glory.

When we read these words, it thrills us to reflect upon the scene that John recorded. We wonder what it would be like to join in that declaration of God's praise. We long for an experience like John's—the privilege of being in the presence of heaven. Yet, this is the wonder of praise. When we proclaim the glory of God, our worship elevates us into the presence of God to join with these angelic beings in announcing God's wonder. To praise God is to be transported into the company of angels. The reason heaven seems so distant to us is that praise is so far removed from our lips. As a result, our vision becomes blinded by the dullness and mundanity of our daily existence. When praise is absent, life becomes hell on earth, for hell is where God's praise is silent.

The more you praise God, the more you will experience the joy of your salvation. If your Christian life seems routine and joyless, look no further than your thoughts and words regarding God. When you fix your mind upon God and proclaim His praises to others, it elevates you from the mundane to the sublime.

Day 4
Submission: The Heart of Worship

Read Romans 11:33–12:2

Present your bodies a living and holy sacrifice, acceptable to God, which is your spiritual service of worship. Romans 12:1

There have been times when the music of praise has brought me an overwhelming sense of worship. Hearing forty thousand men resounding the glory of God together while singing the hymn "Holy, Holy, Holy" or hearing a choir singing the Hallelujah Chorus as the audience stands in honor of God elevates me into the presence of angels. Yet, these moments are few and fleeting. How do we worship God in the mundane aspects of life? It is easy to worship in the thrill of rapturous hymns, but how do we worship God when cleaning the muck out of a barn or doing the weekly laundry? If our life is to be a continual anthem of praise, our worship must encompass both the unpleasant and the euphoric. Worship is a lifelong, moment-by-moment response to who God is and what He continually does for us. Therefore, we are to wrestle with the question, "How does worship embrace all of life's experiences and events?"

Paul provides the answer to this question. Leading up to Paul's anthem of praise in Romans 11:33–36, he has outlined the wonder of God's redemptive work. This doxology of praise is the rapturous response to God's infinite mercy, which He displayed in achieving our salvation from the clutches of sin. Nevertheless, Paul does not relegate praise to just exhilarating moments; instead, in Romans 12:1–2, he expands it to the affairs of everyday life. Praise is not a transient response but an unending life of worship. To highlight what this means, Paul takes us back to the most unlikely place: the bloody altar of death. In doing so, he presents us with a paradox: that we are to be living sacrifice.

We are to be continually living in a place where death reigns supreme. This is the paradox that Christ points to when He states, "Whoever seeks to keep his life will lose it, and whoever loses his life will preserve it" (Luke 17:33). Both Paul's and Christ's point is that true life and freedom are found when we completely surrender our lives to God. In the Old Testament, the sacrificial animal was burned on the altar, thus being wholly dedicated to God. So now we are to live every day in complete, unconditional surrender to God. We are to surrender our dreams, desires, actions, motives, and thoughts to God's absolute control. We are to die to ourselves so that we might find life in Christ. Paul points this out in Colossians 3:17: "Whatever you do in word or deed, do all in the name of the Lord Jesus, giving thanks through Him to God the Father." In other words, whether we are mucking the barn or listening to a choir, we are to do all things in the context of our service and submission to Christ.

This is the essence and heart of worship. Worship is not a service we attend; it is not an event we participate in; it is not a momentary thrill: it is life continually lived. It is a daily, moment by moment, surrendering of our lives to God. Instead of conforming our lives to the worldview of secular culture, we are to adapt our lives to God's will, which is revealed in Scripture. Worship without submission is false worship. When we have surrendered our whole lives, then we truly discover the heart of worship.

Day 5
Praise: The Purpose of Life

Isaiah 43:1–21

The people whom I formed for Myself will declare My praise. Isaiah 43:21

Israel was in the throes of experiencing God's discipline. The Israelites were captured and deported because of their continual rebellion against God and their refusal to walk in obedience to God's law. It was a time when heaven seemed silent, when their lives were in a spiritual wilderness. However, resonating with the words of Hebrews 12:10, Isaiah reminds the people of Israel that the captivity had a redemptive purpose. They were no longer to wallow in the quagmire of past guilt and regret. Instead, they were to look to the future as God rebuilt a new relationship with them (Isaiah 43:18). Thus, God's discipline of His people is not to be construed as a complete rejection.

Instead of forsaking Israel, God brought His discipline to refine and cleanse them. In the end, He will restore them. The trek in the wilderness is not final, for God will bring rivers of refreshment into the barrenness of the desert. To offer proof, He points to the residents of the wilderness that He cares for. The jackals and the ostriches, which live in the wilderness, do so because God provides water and care for them. By their capacity to live in the most barren areas, they give a testimony of God's grace and His provision. Their lives bring glory to God because they serve as a reminder that even in the most inhospitable wastelands of life, God is still present with His people—even when His hand of discipline is heavy upon them (vIsaiah 43:2). They are still precious in His sight, and He will restore them and bring them back to the land again (vv. 4–6). Consequently, in the end, Israel will declare the praise of God (v. 21).

This is what brings us back to our purpose in life. In verse 7, God reminds the people of Israel that He has called them and created them for His glory. In other words, their whole existence finds its ultimate purpose in the praise and glory of God. The same is true for us. We are created to praise God, and we are Saved from sin to bring Him glory. The tragedy is that we can become distracted from this end. In the daily affairs of life, we can become so focused on the present and on the pursuit of our own plans that we forget our real purpose. We pursue dreams that become nightmares as we strive to find meaning, which only leaves us empty. When we live our lives to bring glory to God, we genuinely discover significance and purpose.

Becoming sidetracked in worship is what makes the trials of life so dangerous. The greatest danger, and what should cause us the greatest fear, is not the external struggles we face; it is the danger of spiritual distractions. We can easily slip away into a spiritual wilderness without being aware of it. As a result, we will find ourselves filling our lives with other activities while leaving feeling empty and unfulfilled. We need to remember that our purpose in life is not found in this world's activities but the praise and glory of God.

Do you find yourself growing closer to God or becoming more distant from Him? If it is the latter, then refocus your life upon Christ. "Draw near to God, and He will draw near to you" (James 4:8). This begins with praise.

The Divine Invitation

To honestly know God is not just to know about Him or to see life through the lens of His character; it is to daily experience the reality of Him. It is to walk with Him and grow in a relationship with Him. The invitation to be in a relationship with the triune God can only be realized by accepting Christ's work of redemption on the cross. This begins with first acknowledging our unworthiness and sin. When we act in rebellion against God and break his moral commands—and all of us have—we are worthy of judgment. As Paul points out in Romans 3:23, "For all have sinned and fall short of the glory of God." He further points out in 6:23, "For the wages of sin is death." Every one of us has sinned and now faces the certainty of God's judgment. However, in the desperation of our need, God's grace provides an answer: "But God demonstrates His own love toward us, in that while we were yet sinners, Christ died for us" (Romans 5:8). In other words, Christ, by dying in our place, did what we can never accomplish. He fully paid for our sin and satisfied the justice and righteousness of God. Our salvation is no longer based upon our ability or even our efforts, but solely His grace, "for by grace you have been saved through faith; and that not of yourselves, it is the gift of God;

not as a result of works, so that no one may boast" (Ephesians 3:8–9).

However, His salvation is not universal, for it requires a response on our part. That response is the act of faith by which we trust entirely in Christ and surrender our lives to Him. If we reject Christ, then we face the reality of His judgment. "For God so loved the world, that He gave His only begotten Son, that whoever believes in Him shall not perish, but have eternal life . . . He who believes in Him is not judged; he who does not believe has been judged already because he has not believed in the name of the only begotten Son of God" (John 3:16–18). His salvation is a gift freely offered. However, it can be rejected as a gift, and when it is, then it no longer has any benefit. To rebuff the offer of salvation because we believe we do not need it is to reject the one hope we have. The only appropriate response is to pray this simple prayer:

"God, I understand that I am a sinner, and because of Your righteousness, I am deserving of Your judgment. But I accept by faith that You sent Your Son to die in my place and pay the penalty of my sin. Because of His work, I ask that You save me from my sin and make me one of Your children."

However, God's purpose is not just to save us *from* sin but also *to* an eternal relationship with Him. Eternal life is not just living forever in heaven; it is entering into a lasting relationship with God that begins now and is culminated in heaven. God desires to be a part of our lives. He redeems us to be transformed into the image of His Son. He wants to change us. This change begins when we identify with Christ through baptism and then surrender our lives to Him. To know Christ is to make Christ our supreme desire. There is nothing more we desire than to "gain Christ and [be] found in Him, not having a righteousness of [our] own derived from the law, but that which is through faith in Christ, the righteousness which comes from God based on faith, that [we] may know Him and the power of His resurrection and the fellowship of His sufferings, being conformed to His death so that [we] may attain to the resurrection from the dead" (Philippians 3:8–11).

Our identification with Christ brings us complete newness of life. The old life we live, the one filled with mistakes, failures, and sin, is now put to death, and Christ gives us a new life that is free from the pain of sin (2 Corinthians 5:17). No matter what our former lives were like, no matter how much we failed in the past, God has created us anew and restored in us a life free from the guilt of the past. He now desires to do the one thing that is most remarkable, and that is to conform our lives to His image. The study of the character and attributes of God is not just a study about God; it is also a study of what God desires to share with us. In the wonders of His grace, we become partakers of the divine nature (2 Peter 1:4).

While we may have come to the end of our journey in this book, we discover that we are just starting the journey in His Book—the Book of Life; and that is the most important journey of all. May yours be one constant prayer that you would not just know about God, but that you would experience the complete joy of *knowing* God. When you accept Christ and surrender to Him in all circumstances of life, you discover that He is your Lighthouse. He is the one who provides security and direction in the storms of life to guide you to His safe harbor—your eternal home with Him.

For Further Reading on the Attributes of God

The following books were instrumental in the writing of this book and are recommended for further reading regarding the attributes of God.

Myrna Alexander, *Behold Your God: Studies on the Attributes of God* (Harper Christian Resources, 1978).

Stephen Charnock, *The Existence and Attributes of God* (Grand Rapids: Baker Book House, 1979).

Millard J. Erickson, *Christian Theology*, vol. 1. (Grand Rapids: Baker Book House, 1983).

Millard J. Erickson, *God the Father Almighty* (Grand Rapids: Baker Books, 1998).

Tony Evans, *God, Himself: A Journey Through His Attributes* (Chicago: Moody Publishers, 2020).

Wayne Grudem, *Systematic Theology* (Grand Rapids: Zondervan, 1994).

Thomas C. Oden, *The Living God* (San Francisco: Harper and Row, 1987).

J. I. Packer, *Knowing God* (Downers Grove: Intervarsity Press, 1973).

Arthur W. Pink, *The Attributes of God* (Grand Rapids Baker Books, 2006).

A. W. Tozer, *The Knowledge of the Holy* (Harper One, 1961).

Printed in the United States
by Baker & Taylor Publisher Services